Praise for "Help! I'm Bipolar"

"Very easy to read and understand. Great insights from a patient and clinical perspective. Excellent resource for anyone with bipolar disorder, counselors-in-training, physicians, family members, and loved ones. Kristi's "Help! I'm Bipolar" is the yellow brick road creating opportunities for change and growth in others willing to walk the walk!"

- Dr. Joanne Oestmann, LMHC, LPC, LPCS

"An amazingly clear and brutally honest window into what it's like living with bipolar disorder."

- William Lockhart, LPC

HELP! I'M BIPOLAR

Help! I'm Bipolar

Life Hacks for Us

KRISTI WELDON

HowNowBlackCow

Copyright © 2024 by Kristi S. Weldon

All rights reserved. No part of this book may be reproduced in any manner whatsoever without written permission except in the case of brief quotations embodied in critical articles and reviews.

The material in this book is intended for education. It is not meant to take the place of diagnosis and treatment by a qualified medical practitioner or therapist. No expressed or implied guarantee as to the effects of the use of the recommendations can be given nor liability taken.

First Printing, 2024

To Lee,

From the bottom of my heart,

thank you.

Contents

Dedication — vii
Foreword — xi
Preface — xvii

1	What Bipolar Feels Like	1
2	Good News—or is it?	7
3	Building Your Arsenal: Psychiatric Professionals	16
4	Building Your Arsenal: Medication	26
5	Building Your Arsenal: Therapists	33
6	I Can't Afford This	42
7	The Role of Friends and Family	46
8	Managing Backslides and Self-Care	52
9	The Best and Worst of Times	66
10	The Abyss	73
11	Triggers	83
12	A Different Approach	88

13	Maintenance	93
14	The Workplace	97
15	Bipolar and What Law?	108
16	Hope for the Future	112
17	Taking Control of Your Destiny	117

Appendix A: Questions From Readers — 124
Appendix B: Recommended Reading And Exercises — 129
Appendix C: Additional Resources — 131
Endnotes — 135

Foreword

BY DR. JOANNE OESTMANN, LMHC, LPC, LPCS

My journey in the Mental Health field began when I was 15 and found out my grandmother (Jean Johanna) passed away in a state mental health facility where she was institutionalized and labeled as mentally ill when depression struck subsequently following the birth of her youngest son, my mother's brother. My mother dropped out of High School to raise her two brothers and take care of my grandfather. My passion for psychiatry developed from questions. Why did she have to go into a hospital? Why did she have to live there? Many years later, I'm still asking questions. What other things could have been part of her illness? Was it post-partum depression? Was that fueled by grief and loss of being taken from her family, labeled mentally ill and isolated? Did she have bipolar depression later, causing anger episodes? Did her diabetes contribute to her illness? Consequent amputations? Lack of visitors/family?

It was like everyone, including family, forgot her there, and then she died. Mental health treatment in the 1970s was just beginning to develop as was medicine as we know it today. Where is the compassion, the communication, the research? Was this so scary my own family would not speak of it? There has to be a better way.

My career path presented itself to me, which has included over 45 years in the healthcare and mental health fields as a licensed mental health/professional counselor and supervisor in a variety of settings, from in-patient to partial hospitalization and out-patient treatment centers, and I've enjoyed work as an administrator, clinician, clinical supervisor, and professor specializing in clinical assessment, diagnostics and evaluation with specializations in women's issues, medical psychology, and conjoint couple's therapy. So, what makes bipolar disorder such a hard disorder to see and identify and for those who experience it even harder to live with and embrace?

The face of bipolar disorder is different for each individual, yet many of the troubling subtle symptoms manifest themselves in ways we miss. The lack of boundaries seems engaging; the happiness seems joyful; the swings so subtle one might question if they imagine it, and the anger might even seem passionate at times. Years of family drama that included being the target of 'bipolar rage attacks,' grandiosity, and control expanded to extended family, then clients. Clients in and out of the hospital with highs and lows so extreme we missed the middle part of their daily lives. Years of clinical training and supervision, all the textbooks, and training in diagnostics cannot prepare you for what bipolar looks and feels like in everyday life. I worked with some gifted psychiatrists and therapists along the way to guide my growth journey, and I wanted to be that for others.

The common theme of an emotional revolving door of mood swings, the unpredicted rage without reason, fear, poor judgment, and a lack of insight into what happens before, during, and after these events, as well as the individual being the victim of frequent life crises expanded my passion to learn more on this topic to better support my clients. Books like "A Brilliant Madness" (1993) describing Patty Duke's journey or Dr. Kay Redfield Jamison contributed "An Unquiet Mind: A Memoir of Moods and Madness" (1996), an outstanding book offering dual perspectives from the lens of the physician and patient share narratives about their experiences were the foundation for better understanding the person behind the diagnosis.

Forty-two years later, Kristi walked into my life with her strong, self-assured, well-presented introduction: "I've been in therapy since I was diagnosed with bipolar disorder in 2003. I am dealing with...and I am most comfortable with therapists who are open to...and willing to..." Kristi masterfully asked for specifically what she wanted from a therapist and a partner in her health. She was clear that this was a lifelong journey that she took seriously and was committed to not only doing what she needed to but also would act accordingly. Taking action and creating change is what many miss. Being committed to a lifelong journey, many miss. It is an honor to work alongside Kristi as a partner in her health and joyful to watch her light shine so brightly as she sheds light on a tough topic through the lens of her life view!

"Help! I'm Bipolar" is a toolbox and how-to book for anyone experiencing bipolar disorder, for family, friends, co-workers, and partners. It is a great book for college and graduate school reading lists in clinical programs to bring a real-life perspective on bipolar disorder along with the challenges and hardships. It has helped clients not sure of what is going on in their lives better understand their symptoms and seek help saving marriages, lives, and friends.

Kristi Weldon describes what it feels like in a way that is understandable, applicable, and connected to the current research. She is courageous, passionate, and is a gifted writer and storyteller. Her story is here to help you better understand, feel, and become a better version of yourself. It dispels myths, it reframes, it clarifies, and most importantly, it is a how-to book on taking control of the disease and staying in the driver's seat (Chapters 3-5), forming a strong treatment team, integrative medicine, self-care, self-love, compassion, grace, gratitude and as Kristi so admirably described:

Being real, positive and with attitude taking control of your destiny! Why? Because you can.

Kristi's "Help! I'm Bipolar" is the yellow brick road creating opportunities for change and growth in others willing to walk the walk!

Preface

It took me over ten years to complete this third edition of "Help! I'm Bipolar." I have experienced much more since the first edition, originally titled "What Bipolar Feels Like." I felt it was important to include this new information.

The book is recommended by therapists and psychiatric professionals alike. It's even required reading for some therapists-in-training. In doing the first edition, I reached a point where every time I sat down to write, I would have a breakdown or a breakthrough before I finished a single page.

I was married when I wrote the first two editions and am now divorced. I've done my best to clarify while keeping the essence, but all the "ex-husband"s don't make sense in context. The same goes for my parents, with whom I am now no contact.

Growth is a process. I didn't learn all of this overnight. Don't expect to grasp it that quickly either.

Second Edition Preface

So, I set this manuscript aside and started writing fiction, which I have excelled at sucking since at least fifth grade and most likely before. Now I have learned how to write fiction, and it turns out I'm pretty good at it. I just had to find the right people to teach me how, and my hard work has paid off.

I've carried guilt these years, specifically for not writing this book when I have received emails from bipolar patients and family members alike requesting help and more information. I've answered the specific questions on a case-by-case basis.

Why did I pick up this manuscript again? Augusten Burroughs. Perfectly, today is Easter Sunday, a time of rebirth and new beginnings. Friday morning, I started Burroughs's self-help book, "This Is How: Surviving What You Think You Can't." By Friday afternoon, my paradigms were sufficiently shattered that I took a conscious break before reading the chapter "How to Remain Unhealed." I picked the book up again Saturday morning and finished it around 1:00 p.m.

I am a better person. I am a stronger person. I have more appreciation for myself and for how I want to use my life. I am better equipped to meet some of life's most difficult challenges. And I hope to be a braver person before it's done. But finishing the book about bipolar disorder was on my mind even before, creeping in to peek around the recesses of my brain.

"Come back to me," it called. "I need you. They need you to complete me."

As I sat down on Easter morning and attempted to assuage my guilt of not attending church with the excuse that the incense might trigger my asthma and allergies, I opened my manuscript and continued the erotic novella I was writing as Kristi Hancock. I originally had planned to hide behind the pseudonym and have even obscured most of my face in my pictures. The second reason I chose a pen name was for branding purposes. Let's face it, if you're expecting another book on bipolar disorder and open up to a ménage— or vice versa—it will likely be a disappointment. So out of the closet, I come – I write erotica as Kristi Hancock and contemporary romance as Kristine Bria. Kristi Weldon is my real name, though I have a sister-in-law who can claim the same.

That morning I wrote about two sentences in my story in progress. I wanted my characters to talk to me, to tell me what would happen next. They wouldn't. My mind kept coming back here to this manuscript. I had the pleasure and honor of speaking with Augusten last night. He was tall and humble and engaging and real. When I shared what his book had done for me, he said thank you, of course, but more profoundly, "That's why I wrote it."

That's why I'm writing this. To make you better. To make you stronger. To make you smarter. It's time for me to write it. My heroine has crossed her arms and is tapping her toe with impatience, refusing to let me tell her story until this is done. She is even doing this knowing that I have an editor at a major publishing house waiting to meet her. But this book won't wait.

Whereas I used to work from outlines and notecards, I have learned how to write "by the seat of my pants." That's where much of this is coming from. Do your thinking at the keyboard, or something similar, Augusten said. There I was, with a fierce twenty-six-year-old punk rock girl standing over my shoulder, pushing me to finish this so I could hear her tale.

I have done my best to write the book that wants to be written. Sometimes it will seem contradictory. That is the nature of the beast, as are mania and depression. You may love or hate it. But I can promise you that it will be real.

Chapter 1

What Bipolar Feels Like

Imagine a runaway train. It rolls faster and faster down the tracks until the cars scream on the rails. It approaches a tunnel...and enters safely, though you don't know how. It barrels out the other side and across a bridge. Your breath catches as it speeds even more. And yet, it survives intact. You heave an audible sigh of relief. Until you see the curve ahead. I don't have to tell you what's going to happen. You know it in your soul.

Who is that train? Is it a partner or a parent? A sister or a brother? A child or a friend? Or is it you?

If you have bipolar, you recognize this, though you're not always this way.

Sometimes, you're stable. You're not particularly up. You're not particularly down. You're not agitated.

You're reasonably in control. You're just having a day. This, my friends, is your baseline. It's what we're all shooting for one hundred percent of the time, and if you have bipolar disorder in any form or fashion, you appreciate having it any of the time.

Sometimes, you're trying to hold your life together, or you're a fist breaking your own life into chunks and dust in a swath of self-destruction. You're manic, and you know it. You're vacuuming at 2 a.m., cleaning your already clean house nonstop, and sleeping just a few hours a night. You're fighting the urge to bring home a dog you don't need and coming home with other weird pets they sold you at the pet store instead. You're drinking too much or even doing drugs, maybe to self-medicate. You're hooking up with a different person every single night. You're clicking the checkout button instead of putting back what's in your cart on that website. You're pitching irresponsible ideas at work, like having computer workstations installed where there are no power outlets and doing it with the confidence of Napoleon.

Sometimes, you're expecting to be discarded because you're depressed. You see no hope for your future, no further purpose in your life. Waking up in the morning feels like swimming through leagues of ocean to get to the surface. You're late for work every day. You may bring yourself to shower twice a week.

Yet somehow, some way, you heal yourself and become stable once again...until you have another episode.

If you have bipolar disorder, you know what it feels like. An episode may be triggered by stress or a specific event, or you may just wake up having a "bad day." While everyone has experienced a "terrible, horrible, no good, very bad day," if you're bipolar, it's different. While "snap out of it" may work for the average person, if someone says that to you, they might as well be talking to a wall. Actually, it's even worse because your reaction is beyond your control, and others don't understand how that's possible. So now, on top of your terrible, horrible, no good, very bad day, you are left feeling inadequate, sub-par, and frustrated because you are incapable of turning it off as if you could flip a switch to manage your moods on demand.

Even though they may have the best intentions, with friends like that, who needs enemies? Worse, they are trying to help, yet so many do not seem to understand the downward spiral of emotions that suck you into a black hole. You may not feel like explaining it to them. Even if you do, your state impacts your clarity and your vocabulary. The result is increased frustration because you are unable to get your point across, not that they could relate to it anyway.

Then again, the whirlpool may pull you down until you withdraw within yourself. You don't want to see anyone—friends, family, or even the delivery person. You may screen your calls, "hide" in your home, and stay in your pajamas for days at a time. If you do answer the phone, you make excuses because you know it will simply take too much effort to interact with another person. You may feel physically unwell, which contributes to this vicious cycle. The situation can escalate until you spend days or hours sleeping in bed or becoming a vegetable in front of the television.

If this happens to you, you may or may not care. Neither is necessarily better or worse than the other. If you do care, then you may become judgmental and beat up on yourself, inevitably driving you further into the abyss. If you do not care, then you may not even recognize the need to change your situation.

At the other end of the pole, there are the many variations of mania. Most people don't realize that agitation and irritability are faces of mania, as well as the "happy-happy-joy-joy" they expect as the opposite of depression. Again, while there are many labels, do they really matter? If a "steady state" is your goal, then all the name indicates is either the quantity or quality of "stuff" that you will need to work through to get back to your baseline. And that stuff is different for everyone.

So, what does mania feel like? Often, it feels great. It may feel so great that you don't notice it. Or if you do, you may want to maintain the high simply because it's not a low. You feel brilliant. You feel powerful. You feel in control. You feel productive. You feel important. You can do no wrong. It doesn't take a genius to see why you might want to maintain this state. That is, until you view your actions objectively from your baseline steady state.

As necessary and constructive as that process is, it will likely leave you feeling embarrassed. You may believe you've made an ass out of yourself in front of supervisors, coworkers, friends, family, and strangers. Then you start to beat yourself up again, and into the downward spiral you go.

If swinging between these poles is not challenging enough, some individuals may experience both extremes simultaneously. It can be very confusing not only for you but also for everyone around you. You don't know what to do, and neither do they. It manifests as total unpredictability. This can easily transform into chaos and a churning cauldron of emotions on all sides.

It is difficult, at best, to maintain "normal" relationships while you're dealing with all of this. As you return to a comfortable state of mind, you not only have to pick up the results of any "messes" you may have created during the episode. You are also responsible for apologizing, reconstructing, or writing off any damaged relationships. That's a lot for anyone to deal with. In some ways, it can just seem easier to go hide so you can avoid the entire situation. But I'm not telling you anything you don't already know.

This entire conversation may seem knee–dragging depressing to some of you. However, to borrow a phrase from Dr. Phil, you can't change what you don't acknowledge. Besides, once you've made some progress, don't you want to know how far you have really come? The other main reason why I want to cover all of this is because I want and need you to know that I understand. I've been there. I've done that. And if I can do this, you can do this.

Chapter 2

Good News— or is it?

If you've sought out this book, odds are that you're either bipolar or you know someone who is. This means you're dealing with mood swings and uncontrollable emotional impulses, which can be not only self-destructive but also destructive to those around you. That's not something to feel good about since one study estimates almost four out of every one hundred people have Bipolar I or II.[1] How many people do you know? My point exactly.

How is this good news?

Firstly, you have a diagnosis. You know what the issue is. You can research bipolar disorder through your public library, local bookstore, or the Internet (as with anything, be sure to check the source). If you haven't yet done this, they are great starting points. As they say on School House Rock, knowledge is power. In doing your research, you'll find there are many different variations within a diagnosis of bipolar disorder, and individuals are not easily categorized. For example, you may suffer from symptoms of hypomania or mania and depression—sometimes all at once, which is called a mixed state. I do mixed states really well.

Additionally, many people with bipolar disorder also exhibit symptoms of anxiety disorder, obsessive-compulsive disorder, and attention deficit disorder. Because of this, it is more important for you to know yourself and be able to recognize and identify your symptoms than it is to be able to "label" yourself properly.

The second piece of good news is if you have this diagnosis, you know what your challenge is. Look at the people around you. Look at the people in your life. How many of them are struggling with issues and are in complete denial about it? Within your own family, you may see people with self-esteem problems, co-dependency issues, and behavioral or mental health challenges. As you examine the larger circle around you, you may find rage, addictions, or abuse. You see, we all have our challenges in life. Yours may be different from those of the people around you. But hey, at least you know what yours are.

Thirdly, if you have received this diagnosis, then you have worked with one or more professionals insightful enough to identify the overall disorder instead of getting lost in the barrage of symptoms. Guess what else this means? You have at least started building a professional support network. This will be invaluable to you, and there is no substitute.

A therapist and my primary care doctor diagnosed me with bipolar disorder over twenty years ago at the age of thirty-two. I've been in therapy since then and figure I will be until I die. I've tried a lot of things over those years. I'm not a doctor, I'm not a therapist, and I'm not here to tell you my life story, though I will certainly share my own personal experiences as they relate to the subjects at hand. I will be frank in my opinions, which are just that.

Even if you do every single thing right—you get good rest, take your medication, go to therapy, and work at being stable—life will throw you a curve ball, triggering an episode of epic proportions, and you can go from having a perfectly lovely day to a screaming crying ball of crazy in a matter of moments.

At one point, the water dispenser stopped working in our refrigerator door. It wasn't the end of the world, but when your husband (at the time) had dysentery severe enough to require nineteen IVs, he's allowed to be picky about filtered water. The fridge was under warranty, anyway, so there was no charge. We'd just get it fixed. Right?

Household management generally fell under my purview, so I called, got all the sixteen-digit numbers, and demonstrated the secret handshake so the appliance repairman would come out. Done. Not even an awful wait. He showed up, acting professionally and radiating a confidence that implied he had been doing this for about thirty years. Diagnosis: the water was frozen in the tube in the door. Solution: Replace the left door, which happened to be on backorder for about a month. Temporary solution: Leave the light in the dispenser on to see if the heat would melt the ice and clear the line. That didn't work.

The door arrived early. I called to schedule an appointment, and the professional came back out and replaced the door. Excellent. Except he left the old refrigerator door here. I asked about it as he headed for the door.

"Oh, they'll call you to schedule a pick-up."

"Okay." I was perky. Life was good. My husband had filtered water. Granted, there was a refrigerator door in a giant box on my dining room floor, but that was temporary, right?

Two weeks passed, and I hadn't thought about the situation except in passing, but it was starting to annoy me that they hadn't called. I mean, what kind of customer service is it to leave a busted refrigerator door in someone's living room? So I called them. In her snootiest voice, the sweet young representative informed me, "We don't offer that service anymore."

"But he said..." I explained.

"Well, we don't."

"What am I supposed to do with an old refrigerator door?"

"I don't know. Maybe check with the dump or something?"

Tiffany, the customer service representative, could not have cared less that I had a defective appliance part larger than I am laying on the floor next to my beautiful new dining room set or that I had been waiting for two weeks for them to do something that was never going to happen.

Maybe it was the shock. Maybe it was the total lack of sympathy. Maybe it was the void of accountability that kept her from apologizing for the misunderstanding. In the end, it didn't matter.

After calling for an estimate to have it removed, scheduling the appointment for the next day, and getting an "it's going to start feeling okay" breathing rhythm, my husband exploded. "I'm not paying for that!"

I was back at square one. Worse, actually, because I had generated a solution only to have it shot down. The last time we needed something similar, our trash service didn't provide pick up. We had to drive it to the dump ourselves, almost an hour from our house. Which meant we needed a vehicle to carry it. Which I didn't have.

An hour later, following calls to vent to friends and family who failed to express an appropriate level of outrage at the situation, I cracked. Right down the middle and crumbled into a sobbing heap of uselessness, requiring medication and a total lack of stimulation. It took me days to recover.

I tell you, most of the time when I am triggered, it's by something crazy out of left field that I don't see coming. People with bipolar disorder can do everything right, and then one tiny thing can cause a chemical imbalance that sends them mentally and emotionally over the edge.

A Word about "Recovery"

You might "recover" from manic or depressive episodes, but you never "recover" from bipolar disorder. You manage it. You monitor your symptoms the way a diabetic checks their blood sugar. When you do spiral out of control, you wish there was something as simple as an insulin shot to bring you back into the "normal" range. But there's not.

As I use "recover," it means "to return to a normal state after a period of difficulty."[2] One doesn't "recover" from bipolar disorder any more than they do from asthma. One can "recover" from an episode just like one can recover from an asthma attack. So what does it mean to be "in recovery?" Merriam-Webster describes the state as "the process of combating a disorder (as alcoholism) or a real or perceived problem."[3] The societal connotations, which are usually associated with substance abuse, imply that if one is "in recovery," then they are actively not using whatever substance they're addicted to.

I was struggling with the variety and inconsistency of definitions I found online and from experts and I'm a professional writer who knows some research hacks, so I asked my good friend ChatGPT 3.5 to define it for me. Here's the answer it came back with:

> "Bipolar recovery refers to the process by which individuals with bipolar disorder work towards achieving stability, wellness, and an improved quality of life after experiencing symptoms of the disorder. It involves various aspects such as managing mood episodes, adhering to treatment plans, developing coping strategies, and making lifestyle changes to support mental health.
>
> Key components of bipolar recovery may include:
>
> 1. **Medication Management:** Working with healthcare providers to find the right combination of medications to stabilize mood and reduce symptoms of bipolar disorder.
> 2. **Therapy and Counseling:** Participating in therapy sessions, such as cognitive-behavioral therapy (CBT) or interpersonal therapy, to learn coping skills, manage stress, and address underlying issues contributing to bipolar disorder.
> 3. **Lifestyle Changes:** Adopting a healthy lifestyle that includes regular exercise, balanced nutrition, adequate sleep, and

avoidance of substances like alcohol and drugs that can exacerbate symptoms.
4. **Support System:** Building a strong support network of family, friends, and mental health professionals who can provide understanding, encouragement, and assistance during challenging times.
5. **Education and Self-Management:** Learning about bipolar disorder, its symptoms, triggers, and treatment options, and actively participating in managing one's own mental health through self-awareness and self-care practices.
6. **Monitoring Symptoms:** Regularly monitoring mood changes and symptoms of bipolar disorder, and seeking help promptly when experiencing warning signs of relapse or worsening symptoms.
7. **Goal Setting:** Setting realistic goals for recovery, whether they are related to work, relationships, or personal development, and taking steps to achieve them while prioritizing mental health and well-being.

Bipolar recovery is an ongoing process that may involve setbacks and challenges, but with dedication, support, and effective management strategies, individuals can lead fulfilling lives despite the presence of bipolar disorder. It's important for those affected by bipolar disorder to remember that recovery is possible and that seeking help and support is a crucial step towards achieving wellness."[4]

This is the first time I've seen a definition of bipolar recovery that I can embrace without qualification. That said, I'm sure if I'd seen it when I was first diagnosed, I would have been seriously overwhelmed.

Don't worry about this right now. Put it out of your head for the time being. This book was written well before I saw this definition. And it's a how-to guide for it...if you want it.

I tackled these monster items one step at a time decades ago, and I'm going to tell you how to do it, too. Just kick back and read on.

Chapter 3

Building Your Arsenal: Psychiatric Professionals

In some ways, managing bipolar disorder is a battle—a battle for your quality of life. In order to adequately prepare for the fight, you will need to prepare yourself by gathering appropriate resources. While you are the frontline and will always need to be vigilant, as daunting as that may seem, accept that you cannot and should not be expected to do this by yourself. You need help.

You will also need the ability to identify the right tool for the job. Recognizing what "the job" is will require that you know yourself. That will happen over time. As you become familiar with your resources and as you develop an awareness of your symptoms and triggers, you will learn who you need when.

Journaling can help with tracking this. For example, you can keep a list of your episodes and what happened before them. It may be good or bad news you received, a change in over the counter (OTC) or prescription medication, an argument with someone —it could be anything. There may or may not be a pattern. Or it may take years to detect one, depending on how often you are exposed to the trigger.

For example, I had a reaction to an OTC medication. It sent me into a manic episode after three days. There were no warnings or warning signs. I had taken the ingredients before at the same time but not both of them in the same pill. I went completely manic, not sleeping, pressured speech, going a million miles an hour at everything, and ready to take on the world.

I still don't understand why it happened, but it took months to get my bipolar meds adjusted and stabilize me following the episode. I would not take that medication again if you paid me. This is an example of when you need to see your psychiatric professional.

Lately, I have been receiving a lot of good news. I won an award for my fiction writing. Yay! I've been so excited for so many days that I talked to my therapist because I was afraid that I was becoming manic. My excitement affected my sleep, and I was keeping a close watch on myself for potential symptoms. That's why I see a therapist regularly. In this case, I made a special appointment with her because of these changes. I see her to find out if I am having reasonable reactions and am making reasonable choices as I respond to events in my life. In this case, she said, "No, Kristi, this is normal excitement." But I didn't know if it was or not. That's why I asked a professional who knows me and can counsel me if I need it.

This section explains what professionals I recommend for your arsenal, why you need them, how to find them, and when and how to use them.

Psychiatric Professionals

I have yet to encounter anyone with bipolar disorder who doesn't require some type of medication. That means you need a psychiatric professional, not just a primary care or family doctor, to treat you. Let me tell you about my favorite psychiatrist.

He was an MD, a doctor. He went to medical school. He had hospital privileges, so if I needed to be admitted, he could treat me there. He read scientific journals to keep up with the latest research on mental illnesses and related medications. He attended international conferences so he could speak with other doctors about their research and experiences. He knew which drugs work better if you have bipolar disorder and generalized anxiety, like I do, as opposed to just one or the other. He knew which anti-seizure medications could also work as mood stabilizers. He knew how men's and women's bodies process the drugs differently. He had samples of a wide variety of these medications so that I didn't have to spend $400 to try a new medication that may or may not work. He knew that reducing the dosage of my take-as-needed pills from .5 milligrams to .25 milligrams would resolve the side effects I was having and improve my quality of life. There is no way I would let a primary care doctor treat me for any psychiatric condition on a long-term basis. Just like you need an ENT (ear, nose, and throat doctor) to evaluate if you need a tube in your ear and place it there, you need a psychiatric professional to handle your mental illness.

Psychiatric professionals (as well as P.A.s, D.O.s, and L.N.P.s specializing in psychiatry) are the ones who understand the nuances of bipolar I, bipolar II, mixed states, and rapid cycling. They are the only ones who are well-qualified to treat them.

Even if your regular doctor says they can treat you —and they legally can—would you rather see someone who is treating bipolar disorder a few times a month or someone who is treating it all day, every day? Would you rather see someone who only knows about common drugs or someone who knows about the best treatments for your specific symptoms by following the latest research?

If you were diagnosed with cancer, your family doctor could treat you for that, too. Would you let them? Exactly my point. You want the person who is most knowledgeable about your condition to treat you.

You may say, "My doctor knows me."

Your psychiatric professional will get to know you, too. They ask lots of questions every time you see them. Initially, you probably will see them every two to four weeks.

You may say, "But my doctor said they can treat me, and I don't want to make them mad."

If your doctor gets mad at you because you want to see a specialist to treat *any* medical condition, then you need a new doctor. Period.

Every year I visit my gynecologist for a routine exam. Every year when my (former) primary care doctor gave me a physical, she would try to give me that same exam. Every year I told her, "No. I saw my gynecologist last month. He examines me." Sometimes I would have to say this to the doctor and the nurse after they had the K-Y out and the gloves on. It's annoying, especially if you must repeat yourself, but it's easy. "No." Or, if you want to be polite, "No, thank you."

If I had let her treat me, then I might not have received the best treatment for a condition I didn't know I had. One that required special tests and surgery. My specialist recognized it. He ran tests and gave me four treatment options, two of which were surgeries that my family doctor couldn't have performed even if she did get everything else right.

I'll spare you the suspense: I had a hysterectomy. Best. Decision. Ever.

Bottom line: There are a zillion reasons why specialists are good. Psychiatric professionals specialize in mental illness and (here's the biggie) the medications that treat them. As we have already established, people with bipolar disorder need these medications to make sure they can get out of bed and function, but they aren't so happy that they wind up on the evening news for going on a $30,000 shopping spree. (That really happened to a guy. The people he was buying stuff from said *Hey, this isn't right* and called in help for him. It made the national news. Sadly, it gives us all a poor reputation.)

The most common types of drugs prescribed are antidepressants and mood stabilizers. Just because these are the most common medications does not mean that they are the best fit for you. I recently read an article titled "Emerging Trends: Novel Molecular Targets and Moving Beyond Acute Symptoms in Bipolar Depression" by Eduard Vieta PhD. It was through a continuing education website run by the publishers of "The Journal of Clinical Psychiatry." I can tell you what it means because I have a background in this type of biochemistry. Your family doctor would understand it, too. If they read it. But since they have more patients with heart disease, diabetes, cancer, pneumonia, and the common cold, when do you think they would get around to even subscribing to "The Journal of Clinical Psychiatry"? You know how busy doctors are. When would they find time to read the articles from studies that are done all the time? Why would they if they're only treating a handful of patients with mental health issues? Sure, the drug reps could tell them. But if you were selling psychiatric medications, why would you waste your time pitching to family doctors who might need to write one prescription for your product every three months as opposed to psychiatric professionals who might write several each week? You wouldn't. I have just demonstrated the fact that I, as an author sitting behind my desk researching this book, now know more about the approach scientists are taking with new bipolar medications than your family doctor does because I can guarantee you that at least 99% of them have not read the article or the studies cited in it.

This is why it is crucial to find a psychiatric professional who can appropriately address your needs. Your psychiatric professional should:

Evaluate your history and symptoms,

Prescribe medications to address your symptoms,

Check your progress regularly until you are stabilized, which may include testing different medications and dosages,

Call you back or give you an appointment if something has changed and you are having other psychiatric problems or if your meds aren't sufficiently addressing your symptoms.

You should be aware that your doctor will watch you for warning signs that you don't even realize are potential symptoms of an episode. For example, missing an appointment can be a symptom—even if it is an accident. So can the way you speak. They will ask you different questions to see if you're having an episode based on what they observe. Don't be offended. This is their job. Never forget that they took an oath to heal you. If you become upset by something they ask (and to get a full picture, they will need to ask you very personal questions), the proportion of your outrage in response to the question will be evaluated as a potential symptom. You *want* them to do this because they know more than you do, and they notice things that you don't. While you are in the moment acting and reacting, they are an outside observer, sort of like a journalist. Only when they get the full picture can they make the best decisions regarding your help, which brings me to the next point.

Tell your psychiatric professional the complete truth. Always. If you're drinking or using marijuana or whatever with your meds (which I don't recommend), let them know how often and how much because it impacts your body chemistry. If you stop taking your meds, tell your doctor *immediately*. If anything different is going on with your body or mind or lifestyle or job or kids or parents or responsibilities or stress or sleep or sex life (yes, sexual activity or lack thereof can be a symptom), tell your psychiatric professional as they may want to adjust your medications. They can't fix something they don't know about.

You should *not* expect your psychiatric professional to:

Immediately take your call or call you back, even if you leave an emergency message; if it's that critical, most psychiatric professionals and therapists will tell you to call 911 or go to the nearest hospital emergency room.

Change your medication because you asked them to (though they should listen to your opinion).

Call in a different medication or dosage to your pharmacy without evaluating you in their office first.

How Do I Find a Psychiatric Professional?

The best way to find a good psychiatric professional is to ask a doctor that you trust who they recommend. It doesn't matter if they are your family doctor or your allergist or your gynecologist or your sister's obstetrician, *if you trust them*. They will know someone, or they will ask around to other doctors and get you the name of one. Or four. But they will help you.

I found my favorite doctor through a therapist. I found the therapist through a psychiatric nurse I went to church with. All of my friends at the time, most of whom were retired and wealthy when I was young and wasn't, raved about Alice (name changed). "You just haven't made it until you've been to see Alice." I was in my late twenties and had not yet been diagnosed. My friends were tired of listening to my whining. Alice didn't take insurance and charged $125 an hour. I couldn't afford to go see Alice, so I didn't.

Fast forward: I move away. I'm diagnosed, see doctors, get therapy. I move back. I need a psychiatric professional.

I couldn't afford to see Alice for regular therapy, but I found the money in our budget for me to see her once. I explained the situation, and we made a list of strategies to get me by until I could find a therapist that I could afford. I also printed out a list of psychiatric professionals that my insurance covered and carried it with me. I showed it to her and said, "Who do you recommend?"

She gave me three names from the list. One was accepting new patients. I was with him for over ten years. He was impossible to read and, for years, barely spoke a word to me that wasn't a question about how I was doing or instructions about my medications. I loved him. We built a relationship on honesty and trust. Every once in a while, he made a joke.

It can take time (I'm talking years) for you to build that kind of dynamic with your psychiatric professional. After all, what we say and how we say it can be symptoms of our illness without us knowing it. Scary, eh? It also takes complete truthfulness. Be ready to give that because I wish the same for you.

I highly recommend Psychology Today's website for locating a professional. It is searchable by location, insurance, type of professional, type of therapy, etc., and is well-established. I found my therapist there.

Chapter 4

Building Your Arsenal: Medication

If you have a chemical imbalance, how do you fix that? By adding more chemicals. Welcome to your life on psychiatric medications, also known as psych meds. They can improve your quality of life immensely if you let them. They aren't perfect. One time, you might wind up taking something with five kinds of horrible side effects. Another time you'll think your doctor has prescribed you a miracle drug. It might cost you as little as five dollars or as much as twenty-five hundred. I discuss options for managing costs in the next section.

Your medications will not work like ibuprofen does. It usually takes about a week to get the drug steady in your system and another for your body to adjust to it. That's why it takes at least two weeks to see results. Some, like me, may see them faster, and others may take longer. Assembling the right "cocktail" of meds for your system is an art as much as it is a science. Expect trial and error. Expect that it may take months to get your medications and dosage just right because you aren't only trying to determine which medicines work best with your body chemistry but also how much of them to take and how often to take them. Expect side effects and be prepared to live with some of them. Would you rather gain a few pounds, have a slight tremor, and be stable, or would you rather be hospitalized for mania or depression? If you'd rather be hospitalized, stop reading because this book is a waste of your time. It won't help you because you don't want to be helped.

You manage your illness proactively to prevent episodes and reactively to get back to your "normal" from them, though quite honestly, sometimes you get bounced into a pendulum effect for months before you can fully pull out of an episode. Again, that can happen when you're doing everything right. I should know because it happened to me. That reaction to the new OTC medicine happened in April and left me out of sorts and tweaking bipolar medication with my psychiatric professional through that November. It took seven months to control my symptoms following three or four days of disruption.

You know what you're dealing with. You know that

this can take a while. Seriously, it can take years to find the perfect combination of meds to treat your symptoms. It may take more than one doctor. It may be frustrating. It may be aggravating. It may be depressing. But you have to keep at it. Eventually, you can feel better.

My "eventually" came three days after I was first diagnosed. I was very, very lucky that the first medication my doctors tried worked. That wasn't the end. There were additions, subtractions, and adjustments. Sometimes I developed other weird symptoms that had nothing to do with my mind. One pill made me larger; one pill made me small. One pill made me dizzy in the time-release form, but it worked fine by itself. One gave me tremors so severe that even at the drive-thru, cashiers repeatedly asked, "Are you okay?" In other words, "Should you be driving?" I sounded like a broken record. "I'm fine. It's my medication." No one believed me. We changed my meds.

Now I have some slight memory issues, but I'm able to work, my moods are pretty stable, and I'm generally happy. I discussed it with my psychiatric professional, and we agreed that I'm doing really well and that my side effects aren't bad enough for us to risk changing how well I'm doing. After all, if we change something, I could become manic or depressed. It's not worth the risk. Right now, I see her every three months. Life isn't perfect, but it's pretty darn good.

There is tremendous variance in bipolar patients taking their meds. Depending on the length of time you're measuring (say one month as opposed to several years), 20-60% of patients do not take their medications like they're supposed to.[5] Their attitudes and behaviors are the biggest factors in whether or not people take their meds, even more so than side effects.[6] Whose job is it to stay on top of the medication situation? Yours. Why should you care? If you like to visit the psych ward of your local hospital for regular seventy-two-hour minimum stays, then I guess it doesn't matter. I would rather you not land there if you don't need to.

So, take your medications as prescribed.

"How am I supposed to do that?" you ask.

Make it hard to miss your medication. Go to the pharmacy and buy a pill organizer. I use one with labeled a.m. and p.m. compartments for each day of the week. The days pop out individually, so if I'm having dinner out with a friend on Tuesday night, then I can take Tuesday's pills with me and not have to carry the whole thing.

Every week, make time to set up your pills for the next week. If you need to cut some of your pills in half, buy a pill cutter. They sell those at the pharmacy, too. If you can't find them, just ask someone who works there. They will help you.

Divide up your pills by morning and evening for each day and load the compartments appropriately with your daily doses. Don't get your pills mixed up as you're doing this. Pay attention and stay focused. Ask for help from a friend or family member if you need it. When my tremor is bad, I ask someone to help me.

I bought a pill cutter with a protective panel to keep me from accidentally cutting myself. I switched my pharmacy because I preferred the way they label their prescription bottles. Little things like that can make your life easier. This isn't the only way to manage it, but it's a place to start. My way works for me, but it may not work for you. Don't be afraid to experiment. I still haven't found the perfect time to fix my pill container. I mostly hate doing it, especially since I have a tremor. That always makes it especially fun to chop tiny things, but I do it. I moan, grumble, and complain about it, but I do it because the results are better than if I don't.

When you're done, you have all your pills ready for the week. Over time, memories of taking your pills will blur together in the same way that some days you stop and think, *wait—did I put on deodorant?* If you can't remember whether or not you took your pills, just check your container. There are also lots of great pill reminder apps.

Even doing all this, I will still occasionally miss a dose. At some point, your body may become attuned enough to how it feels with your medication that you may notice if you miss a dose. I experienced that with one of mine. It's good and bad because I can catch my errors because I feel like crap. I try not to miss a dose because I don't want to feel like crap.

Speaking of feeling well, you feel well *because* of

your medication. One of the main reasons bipolar patients end up in the hospital is because they just decide to stop taking their meds. Get ready. You will likely think this, too.

1. You feel better because of your meds.
2. You stop taking your meds because you feel better.
3. You have a manic or depressive episode because you were only better because you were taking your meds.
4. You are hospitalized because you spiral out of control.

Your psychiatric professional(s) (now you might have more than one because the odds of your doctor being on call at the hospital you go to when you go there are slim to none) put you on medication again.

You start over with medication and see your psychiatric professional every two weeks to monitor your progress again.

I did this with the exception of number four. Instead, I was in my bed, hiding, quite literally, with the covers pulled over my head. I made appointments with my psychiatric professional and therapist and dragged my husband to them with me. I sat in their offices and bawled my eyes out, apologizing for going off my medications. It was not a fun experience. I do not recommend it.

If you want to know more about non-adherence

to medication (not taking it as prescribed) and bipolar, please visit http://www.ncbi.nlm.nih.gov/pmc/articles/PMC3691269/ so you can read more about it. This link is to an article entitled "Improving treatment adherence in bipolar disorder: A review of current psychosocial treatment efficacy and recommendations for future treatment development."[7] The authors looked at many different scientific studies and compiled that information in one article. It's free.

Chapter 5

Building Your Arsenal: Therapists

Therapists have different titles, but they all do essentially the same thing. Psychologist. Licensed Professional Counselor (LPC). Licensed Clinical Social Worker (LCSW). Licensed Marriage and Family Therapist (LMFT).

I believe in using a separate psychiatric professional and therapist. The reason for this is if your psychiatric professional works with you on medicine and talk therapy, they are going to be better at one than the other. I want the best of both.

My psychiatric professional does medication only. He wants to know how I'm doing so he can make sure my medications are working properly and that we don't need to change them based on something else going on in my life, like if I changed jobs or was moving—outside stress factors. He doesn't coach me on how to handle situations. He doesn't teach me how to handle stressful situations. He doesn't help me fix the relationships that are imploding because of my erratic behavior. My therapist does all that. My psychiatric professional manages my medications to help control my mood swings. Period.

My therapist helps me deal with my mood swings because no matter how good my psychiatric professional is, they will never completely go away. She gives me an objective opinion on if I am having reasonable (not *normal*, I said *reasonable*) reactions to what is going on in my life. She gives me strategies to improve my quality of life. She sees me much more often than my psychiatric professional does now that I'm relatively stable. She asks me if she thinks I need to call my doctor because she believes I'm having an episode. She also tells me what I am doing right.

She knows the symptoms of mental illnesses, too, but she isn't a doctor. I visit her for an hour at a time. I try to go at least once every two weeks, but if I have stressful events happening, I see her every week if I can afford it. I would not go more than a month without seeing my therapist. I used to think it was a luxury, that I couldn't afford one. The reality is that I can't afford *not* to have one. When I don't visit one regularly, then I don't have a professional to keep all the stuff that makes up my "life" in perspective. Then

I start to think about some things a little too much because I don't know if I'm making the healthiest decisions for me. If I can't function, then I can't work. It's cheaper to see her than not to.

I'm yelling at my cats over things that aren't their fault. I'm angry and irritable. Is my calendar overloaded? Am I stressed out because I'm trying to do too much? Which things should I do? Which things should I not do? How do I say "no" to this person when I owe them a favor? These are the kinds of situations that therapists help you deal with, practical everyday stuff that directly affects your moods. It's not all about letting your inner child speak about when Bobby hurt your feelings on the playground in kindergarten. It's about handling whatever is making you happy or sad or angry or hurt or frustrated right then so that you do not get too happy and have a manic episode or get too upset and have a depressive episode. It's about getting advice for dealing with your friends and family and bosses and coworkers, so you don't accidentally kill relationships. It's about preventing mood swings. It's about helping your medications increase their effectiveness because there is less variation for them to compensate for. It improves your overall quality of life. You will spend less money visiting your psychiatric professional because you won't need to see them as often since you are more stable. That also means your meds won't need to be adjusted as often, which means you won't be having fun discoveries like "this medicine makes me grind my teeth" and "this one makes me sleep for at least ten hours every night." Every time that happens, you and your doctor have to decide whether or not you should live with the side effect or try another medication. See how it all works together?

Here's what you should know about therapists:

1. **You may need to see more than one before you find the right fit.** I make a point to speak with them online or by phone before I even make an appointment. Have a list of specific questions for them, including, "Do you treat patients with bipolar disorder? How?" Also, include your belief systems. For example, I'm a practicing Episcopalian, and I also embrace Tibetan Buddhism (you know, the Dalai Lama?). It's important to me that my therapists know what they're getting in me as a client and if they're a fit for me. There is no single correct answer, but if you aren't comfortable with their answer, then move on to another one. If you're comfortable with their responses, make an appointment and see how that goes. If you get along, then great, you've found your therapist. If not, keep looking. The Psychology Today website (www.PsychologyToday.com) is a great resource and how I found my current therapist. There are many other great resources for online and in-person therapists out there, as well.
2. **Everything you say is confidential, just like**

with a doctor. However, I give my doctor and my therapist each other's contact information so that if it is in my best interest for them to speak to each other, they can. (You will have to sign a form for them.) There is one big fat exception: if they are afraid you are going to hurt yourself or someone else, then they are required to act on it so that does not happen. You may not realize it at the time, but that is what you want them to do. Better to see your doctor or the inside of an emergency room than the inside of a jail cell.

3. **Do not expect them to be on call for you.** If you have a big emergency, some huge event that triggers you into a tailspin, then you should call and tell them. This should not be done more than once every six months if that happens. I've been in therapy for over ten years and have made maybe five of these calls. If you need to call them every week or two, then you need to book more frequent appointments with them. Many therapists will not correspond by email beyond discussing appointments. This is for your protection as well as theirs, as they cannot guarantee privacy. In short: do not abuse your therapist.

4. **Be completely honest with them.** If you aren't, they can't help you. In this case, it's like you're drowning, but because you're not truthful with them, they don't know how far you are from the boat or in which direction to throw the life

preserver. You will make mistakes in life because every single person does, bipolar or not. When you do, tell them. They are not there to judge you. (If they do, go back to item 1 because if they do, you need a different therapist.) They will talk to you about it to help you understand why and how it happened so that you hopefully don't do it again. Really, the only way that you can get in trouble in therapy is by lying, but even then, they will just ask you why you didn't tell them the truth.

5. **Do not expect them to do the work for you.** This is your life; you are driving. You can't just show up once every week or two and be like, *yeah, my life sucks*, and then discuss why it sucks and how to make it suck less but do nothing when you leave. If you do that, in a week or two, you will be back in their office discussing why your life still sucks. It's a waste of time and money. It's also shooting yourself in the foot because you won't feel better. If you are not comfortable making the changes you've discussed together, say so. That's different. "I'm not ready to do that" and "I need to think about that" are perfectly appropriate responses when that's the case. So is "I disagree with you because..." It's their job to help you, not to bully you into doing something you don't want to do.

There is one more topic I need to address. I am

a Christian, but I do not believe in Christianity- or any other religion-based therapy in the treatment of mental illness. Your priest or rabbi may do great marital counseling, but they are not the right person for a bipolar patient. From what I have seen and heard from patients who have used this kind of counseling, I do not believe that there is enough emphasis placed on personal accountability. In other words, I believe there is too much emphasis placed on beliefs and prayer. This is coming from a woman who sometimes prays fifty times a day, mind you. I come from a long line of ministers and have served on church boards, etc. Find a non-religious-based therapist. Ask them about this on the phone or check their website. You aren't looking for an atheist; it doesn't matter if they are Christian, Buddhist, Hindu, Jewish, Pagan, or Zoroastrian. The point is that you don't need someone telling you that you aren't getting better because you haven't prayed hard enough, or you don't believe in someone's teachings strongly enough.

Seriously, think this through with me. Let's say something bad just happened to me at work. My budget got cut, and I have to fire someone. This is an obvious trigger for a depressive episode. How is someone who takes a religious approach to therapy going to guide me through this crisis? Would we examine scripture or writings? Would we discuss what Jesus or Moses or Buddha would do? That may help me discern a way to execute the task, but how do I live with the guilt? Pray about it, which is great, but I would do that anyway. I don't need a therapist to tell me to pray harder. I want a therapist to tell me something to do to give me some semblance of control. By praying, I am asking a higher power to resolve an issue that I should address myself. By all means, pray and study religious texts in addition to your therapy if you are so led, but that should not be your primary solution to managing thoughts and behaviors that are driven by a chemical imbalance in your brain. If it did work, everyone would simply pray their illnesses away, and none of us would need doctors.

This is the part where someone says, "But," and tells the story of someone who was miraculously healed from something. Miracles happen, but if they happened regularly, we would call them something else. Quite honestly, if you experience a "miraculous healing" from bipolar disorder, it is a gigantic red flag that you are having a manic episode, and it's only a matter of time until your world implodes, then you're booking emergency appointments with your psychiatric professional and your therapist and crying your apologies to them, swearing to them that you will never, ever, ever go off your meds again.

I had a friend who went to her pastor for marital counseling by herself after her husband left her. She believed that if she prayed hard enough, then her marriage would be saved, and her husband would be home by Christmas. It didn't happen. I'm not sure what she tells herself about why.

There have been many positive changes in counseling since the 1980s. It has evolved from "cultural awareness" to "cultural humility." This means that your therapist may ask you questions about your life and culture to better understand you. This is a great sign because it means they want to get to know you better and meet you where you are.

However, if your therapist keeps bringing up things that you don't believe in or that make you uncomfortable, they are not upholding their ethical responsibility to you. At that point, it is your responsibility to find a new therapist. Do not feel guilty. Be honest with them because they need this feedback. You do not have to call them out as being unethical but do tell them what they are doing that is making you uncomfortable. If you do not have trust in your therapist, then you might as well burn the money you are spending on them.

We can't afford not to take charge of our own well-being. We are starting at a disadvantage, but that's okay because we know what it is. Accept responsibility. Do whatever you can to make healthy (not "good" and "bad" but "healthy" and "unhealthy") decisions.

Personal accountability is a major theme in this book, so if you disagree with me on this point, I'm not sure how much help I'll be to you overall. If you abdicate responsibility in one area, why wouldn't you in others? And then where are you? Not where I want to be.

Chapter 6

I Can't Afford This

You also can't afford to lose your job or your family or your home because you didn't seek treatment. I've had emails from readers with problems finding an affordable doctor near them. While every case is going to be different, everyone needs to see their psychiatric professional as recommended—and if you can't afford their fee, ask if you can work out a schedule for you to come less often (do this when you're in their office scheduling your next appointment) or if they will work with you on a payment plan or reduced rate. Also, know that while they will need to see you at least every two to four weeks as a new patient, they will not always need to see you that often. It will take time and will vary by individual, but once you are stable (not having an episode because your medications are working well), they will require visits you less and less frequently.

When I am stable, my psychiatric professional sees me every six months. If we change my medications, he will have me come in two to four weeks so we can talk about how they are working and whether or not we need to make another adjustment. Depending on the change and how I'm doing, it's like starting over. The good news is doctors will give you samples (if they have them), so you aren't paying for medication that may change in two weeks. Every little bit helps.

They want you to see them so they can treat you. They want to keep you out of the hospital just like you do. Call the drug companies. Your doctor will usually give you a coupon if there is one—if they exist, the drug company representatives will make sure the doctors have them. You can visit the drug manufacturer's website to research if they have programs for new patients there. Ask your pharmacist. Call your insurance company. Don't change medications just because of what their doctors say, though they may suggest alternatives that you can run past your doctor. Don't give up. Ask questions and be proactive.

The next time you sign up for insurance, consider your total costs. This will be different for everyone. Look at your past year's expenses for doctor visits and medications and run the numbers through a calculator or spreadsheet for each of your choices. I did that, and it's how I chose my plan. While none are perfect,

I use the one that is the cheapest for me based on my medical expenses.

I get the problem. Don't think I don't. I have switched insurance companies through work several times through the years. At one point, my co-pay for a follow-up doctor's visit was as much as if I didn't have insurance at all.

If you don't have insurance, there are some options. Most communities have mental health clinics where people can get a full range of mental health services based on a sliding scale. Sliding scale is where you pay based on your income. Sometimes, this is as little as zero dollars. The primary issue here is that if you are in a rural area, it can mean a considerable drive to the services. The good news is that if you have a change in status to your insurance or Medicaid, you do not usually have to change providers because most of them will accept the payment from them. This can be a game-changer for your care. Please see my resources section to assist you in your search.

While some of my medications cost less than $5 —those would be generics of drugs that have been around for a while—I have paid over $900 for two months of one of my medications. The manufacturer has a special program for it as it's a relatively new drug, but I don't qualify because it's only for patients who are new to the drug. I was already on it. I sucked it up and found the money when I had to because it worked really, really well for me, and there wasn't a substitute. Once I hit my annual deductible and my insurance started paying for it, I had it filled as often as I could.

Sometimes, if you've tried the alternatives to more expensive drugs, but they haven't worked or you've had extreme side effects, your doctor can complete a "Prior Authorization Form" or "Drug Form" (different companies require different forms) for the insurance company for them to cover the expensive drug if it's not on their "approved" list. Don't ask me how those lists work. I could guess, but I don't know for sure. That's not what I'm here for. I'm here to tell you to talk to your doctor and your insurance company in case my experience can help you.

You don't want you in the hospital. *They* don't want you in the hospital. Respectfully and politely explain your financial situation and ask questions so you can see your psychiatric professional and get your medications. Because if you don't, the odds are pretty good you will wind up in the hospital at some point. Ultimately, it is *your* responsibility to prevent that.

Chapter 7

The Role of Friends and Family

Telling your friends and family (whether biological or chosen) that you have bipolar disorder may be one of the scariest things you ever do. *What will they do? How will they treat me? Will my partner leave me?* I don't have children, so I'm not sure how I would explain it to them. When I had an episode in front of my young nephew, I explained to him that I was sick, but instead of sneezing, sometimes I cried. He accepted that fine. Better than my mom and sister, actually.

The day I was diagnosed, I had left my graduate classes early and gone straight to the doctor while on the phone with my therapist because I was having a passive suicidal meltdown. I wanted a truck to take me out so I didn't have to actually kill myself, but I would be dead. When I explained to the doctor what was going on and that my therapist thought I was bipolar and that I had planned to come in the next day anyway, it didn't take very long to get a diagnosis or medication to hold me over until I could get to a psychiatric professional.

I remember sitting on our sofa in our living room, plotting ways to explain the diagnosis to my husband of seven years. I would draw a flat line in the air followed by a mathematical sine curve. I would draw lines marking the tops and bottoms of the wave, showing how wide the range of my current mood swings was compared to how much narrower I hoped they might be. They will never be the straight line that is, essentially, my husband's persistent state. He was my rock of Gibraltar.

When he arrived home from work, I gave my prepared speech, including hand signs. He took it in stride and basically responded, "Okay." Which was a more awesome response than I had hoped for. Quite honestly, I was afraid that since his mother had it and since they were relatively estranged he might leave me. He didn't. When I asked him about his reaction to this book, he confessed that he wasn't surprised and that it didn't really change anything for him. He may not have been surprised by my news, but I was shocked by his reaction or, rather, his lack thereof.

Over ten years later, he would occasionally make some boneheaded statement about me needing to learn how to control my reactions to things. This was usually at a point when I needed to have my meds adjusted. Instead of fighting with him, I just knew that he was wrong because he didn't get it because he didn't have bipolar. After my meds were adjusted, I would thank him for hanging in there with me while I was freaking out, and we would discuss what changes were made, as well as what my psychiatric professional and I hoped they would do. We would hug and feel better. That didn't mean I didn't vent to my therapist.

I waited weeks to tell my parents about my diagnosis and only did so in person when I could hand them a book about it. They harbored a ton of guilt for not catching it earlier. In all fairness, they knew something was off, but when they compared my behavior to that of friends and extended family, it turned out that they were ultimately diagnosed with forms of bipolar, also.

Telling people that you have bipolar disorder is a coming-out process and should be handled as such. There is no right or wrong way to share. You may not want to tell anyone. It's your choice. Some friends may be very supportive and ask what they can do to help. Others may be scared or feel awkward around you. That is their problem to own, not yours. You will likely experience both.

Since I write about bipolar disorder under my real name, I have come out of the closet big time. I am an ambassador for people with bipolar disorder, whether

I want to be or not. Once, I was at a meeting for a writers organization. When I mentioned that I was bipolar to the gentleman (and I use that term loosely) that I was speaking with, he actually looked me up and down and then made a show of moving his chair several inches away from me. I kept going as if it had never happened because I wanted to model positive, stable behavior. He was an asshole, and I won't forget it. But when we stepped away from the conversation, which involved a third person, he was the one who looked rude and ignorant, whereas I looked rational and calm. That is sweet revenge in and of itself. If I had called him out or started an argument—however valid that position might have been—he could say, "See? I told you." As it was, he looked like the jerk I suspect he is.

That same man gave me advice to change something in my manuscript; I thought he was wrong and didn't do what he suggested. My manuscript won an award, and an agent said it was "perfect." I'm not rubbing that in his face, either, even though I would love to do it. I'm an ambassador for bipolar and mental illness, like it or not. If I can control my behavior, then I do because when I can't, oh, it's ugly.

On the flip side, at another meeting, I sat with a group of three other ladies in the same writers group. Over breakfast, I took my meds and explained what they were for. Their response was completely different. One's first response was, "How wonderful that you take your medication." I told them I write bipolar self-help, and they could not have been more supportive. It made me feel really good that I had said something.

You will experience extremes. You don't have to be as open about it as I am. In some situations, such as around my former husband's bosses and employees, I would simply say that wrote self-help. I didn't want them to judge him or me based on any health issues. Granted, when we went to Las Vegas for a few days with a small group from his office, I had an episode, had to leave the dinner table, and spent the evening in the fetal position crying in a chair in our room wrapped up in a blanket. My husband and I told them the truth, and they never mentioned it again. They just went on like nothing happened. I was stunned and thrilled that they knew me well enough not to judge me by it.

The best advice I have for sharing your diagnosis (if possible, which is not always the case) is to:

- Be calm. They may be shocked, and you don't want to contribute to their anxiety.
- Be honest. Don't play it up or play it down. Just give them the facts.
- Tell them what they can expect. You'll be on medications and in therapy. Share your plan and what you and your team hope to accomplish. Let them know that you hope to get "better" and have fewer episodes; they need to understand bipolar disorder does not go away.

- Give them time to process it. It may or may not overwhelm them.
- Tell them how they can help you.

I have friends that I tell when I know I have stressful times coming up and let them know I will need more phone or in-person support. Most are willing to make themselves available to me.

Most importantly, *let* them help you if they can do it in a positive way.

Chapter 8

Managing Backslides and Self-Care

Once you've tumbled down the emotional spiral, the mere thought of trying to function can be daunting. What's the best way to start? Focus on one step at a time. Baby steps count, too.

Find one thing to do that would make you feel better. Since you're already so low and down on yourself, there should be a ton of things you can do that will make you feel at least a tiny bit better than you feel right now. It might be a doughnut, a bubble bath, listening to birds, scratching your dog, playing a favorite song, watching a favorite TV show, watching a mindless TV show, re-watching a favorite movie, getting a massage or manicure or pedicure, walking for 10 minutes, getting dressed in a favorite T-shirt or outfit, or re-reading a favorite book or magazine. It may be different every time. Sometimes you need to "check out" with an escapist tactic to stop beating yourself up. Other times you may need to treat yourself to perk you up a little. You might need to be around "someone" but don't feel fit for human company; nature and pets are great for that.

The point is to pick one thing, just one thing, and do it. Do you know why? Once you've done that, you have set a goal and accomplished it. Even if it was eating a Bavarian cream doughnut, you have decided that you are worthy of happiness and demonstrated it with a specific action. I'm not suggesting burying yourself in a dozen crullers. Food can be as addictive as alcohol, drugs, and gambling, so don't overdo it.

There is one thing you shouldn't try that many people may suggest: positive affirmations. It turns out that people who are suffering from depression actually feel worse about themselves after using these.[8] (Examples include repeating statements such as "I am lovable" or "I am worthy.") If anyone tries to argue this point with you, feel free to tell them about this Canadian study (see the footnote for details) or just say "Thank you" and move on. However you choose to handle it, I recommend listening to the research and not unnecessarily berating yourself, which is what ultimately happens in your psyche if the tactic backfires.

Please note that at other points in this book, I

make some specific suggestions about attitude and ultimately try to move toward a positive one. I recommend you start where you are and try to move to a more neutral thought pattern first, if possible. If you feel the need to wallow in your depression for a while, and you may, then keep reading.

One of my therapists said I don't look back enough. When I do, I tend to focus on my failures. When she looks back with me, she sees how far I've come, shows me the ways in which I've grown, and now feel better.

2011 was a blur except for the anxiety attack I had in February and living with my crumbled self in the aftermath. I see myself smiling in the summer —did we take a vacation? I remember. My husband surprised me with a lovely trip to California. He had been putting it together in his head for years, and it showed. I felt special. We walked by the water and ate at his favorite restaurant. He drove us two hours so I could eat a meal from a chef whose food I fell in love with on TV. We always have great vacations, and this was special among those standards.

What I didn't understand was why I couldn't seem to carry that joy with me. That's when I remembered: I was bipolar and obviously in the midst of a depressive episode.

We had just bought a beautiful new house, and I felt as though I was struggling to push off the ground and crawl one step forward on my hands and knees across the carpet. Before I could finish feeling good about the house, my inner voice chimed in, saying,

"You didn't have anything to do with it." Which was true. I hadn't held down a job or earned any significant amount of money within the past year.

I lived in a house I loved, in a community I loved, with people I loved. Why couldn't I enjoy it? I'm bipolar, and I'm in a depressive state.

Judging myself makes it worse. It's like twisting the knife that life lodged in my solar plexus.

What have I learned from this little exercise? A new beginning cannot be forced. Regardless of how "appropriate" it may seem to you or anyone else, a new beginning is not a choice. For people like us, we must possess at least a sliver of hope that we believe in. Only then can we make a fresh start. I wish I could tell you how to find that hope. I guess that time is the only solution. Keep going. Keep doing. Keep being.

You know how it hurts. You see a movie, read a book, watch a TV show, or simply wake up, and everything's changed. You're not in your "happy space." You're not in "Zen mode." What happened? Maybe you know. Maybe you don't. Does that matter? Not really. You're in a space of apathy or self-loathing. You don't care enough to cry. You are a failure. There's no point in trying. It just doesn't matter. Nothing does. What do you do now?

Starting Over

Start over.

I'm kidding, right? I mean, really, who has the

energy to start over? What's the point? Do I even want to start over? I don't know. I just don't know. So how could you?

As I wrote this, it was a new year. The perfect time for beginnings. A time of hope for help, happiness, and prosperity. This was supposed to be a hopeful chapter. Yet there I sat, mired in the futility of it all. How could I help you create a new beginning if I couldn't create one for myself? I did the only thing I knew how to do at that point. I led by example.

Music Therapy

I created a simple kick-starter for myself, which helps if I remember to use it. It's a shared Spotify playlist that I call "The 39 Minute Attitude Adjustment". It's no longer 39 minutes long, as it's changed over the years since I first created it. The 39 Minute Attitude Adjustment. It starts with "Poor, Poor Pitiful Me" by Linda Ronstadt. I think it's important to acknowledge where you are and to give yourself the opportunity to have that pity party you most likely need. One day I was about to have a breakdown in my car in the parking lot in front of Target, where I needed to go shopping. I listened to that song eight times in a row before I was able to get out of my car and go in the store without crying.

I created another playlist to try to shut my mind up when I'm freaking out. I call it "Driven to Distraction."

Music helps me. You can see if it helps you.

There are a number of bands that focus on mental health. Number one on my list is Shinedown ("Monsters" - "My monsters are real"), followed by Papa Roach ("Help" - "I think I need help"), and Pop Evil ("Paranoid (Crash & Burn)" - "The voice in my head is a threat"). These speak to me.

Find music that speaks to you and use it when you need it. I'm a huge fan of Spotify because you can control what you hear when you need it, one song at a time, in order, on your phone, in your car, on Alexa, or on your television. You can repeat, shuffle, etc. However, you can also play music on any other number of apps. Find the one that best meets your needs and use it to your best advantage.

Managing a Crisis and Proactive Care

Maybe there's something else. Maybe there's someone else. Your support network is always a great resource, but they may not always be available. You need to have a plan that includes things you can do on your own so that when you catch the beginning of a depressive episode, you know you have the power to at least try to intervene before it escalates.

Will it work? I don't know. What works for one person may not work for another. What works for you one time may not help the next time.

Sometimes it helps just to sit and be with the emotions. Sometimes it helps to figure out if there was a trigger and if so, what it was. Processing your emotions can help. "Process" is a psychologist's word. I see it as swimming through the rapids until you eventually reach calmer waters.

Regardless of where you are, you will need to take an active role in your healing on an ongoing basis. Some ways of doing this include:

- **Journaling** - Get a cheap composition book and pen from your local store and go to it with a stream of consciousness. Date the pages in a way that you can look back and identify triggers if needed. Check out "The Artist's Way" by Julia Cameron for Morning Pages to learn how to "take out the trash" in your brain every morning.

- **Exercise, Tai Chi, or yoga** - Explore apps, DVDs, or websites for whatever kind of exercise appeals to you and is approved for you by your physician. Go for a walk. I keep a deck of yoga cards on hand just to pull some random poses to do when I get stressed.

- **Meditation** - I'm a huge fan of the Calm app, specifically the "Daily Jay" by Jay Shetty. You can check him out on YouTube and see if he's a good fit for you. They also have sleep stories and midday meditation reminders.

- **Grounding** - You can sit or lie on the ground or floor to feel the earth's energy. This is totally free and can be done indoors as well as outdoors.

- **Breathing Exercises** - I've been doing and teaching box breathing for years—then I found out that it has a name, and Navy Seals do it. Breathe slowly. Inhale-two-three-four. Hold-two-three-four. Exhale-two-three-four-five-six-seven-eight. Repeat. And keep repeating it until you feel better or get sick of doing it. If the latter happens, you probably need to try something else.

- **Venting** - Find someone in your support system and let them know you just need them to lend an ear while you get your frustrations out verbally. Let them know you're "venting" and are not looking for advice.

- **Temporary escapism** - This could be reading a book or watching TV or a movie. Try to pick something that will not put you in a worse state than when you started. For example, do not watch "Saving Private Ryan" when your prized pet has run away.

- **Visualization** - Use your imagination. Close your eyes (not while driving, watching the kids, etc., of course) and see if you can smell the ocean or a green meadow or freshly baked cookies. What scent will calm you down today? After you identify that, construct the images around it.

Another option is a life jacket or a safety line. This still requires some active participation on your part. However, it involves the use of external support tools. You may want to try one of the following:

- **Acupuncture or Reiki** - Acupuncture is invasive. Reiki is not. I like both, depending on my mood. Both involve others shifting your energy flow.

- **Massage** - This can be very relaxing. There are different kinds—Swedish, Deep Tissue, and Hot Stone—are among the most common. Which one works best for you will be a matter of personal preference.

- **Talk Therapy with your therapist** – This focuses on thinking skills.

- **Cognitive Behavioral Therapy (CBT) with your therapist** -This can work on thoughts and behaviors, as well as coping skills.

- **Dialectical Behavior Therapy (DBT) with your therapist** – This is a modified form of CBT that focuses more heavily on emotions and their regulation.

If You Still Need Help

If you still need help, you can ask for a "life raft." At this point, you're in a place where you're incapable of helping yourself and need to be saved by an outside party. This doesn't mean that you're weak or helpless. In fact, you're in a place of power simply because you know to ask for help. This is a demonstration of knowledge and self-awareness, not shame. May have reached the lowest of lows or the highest of highs, and you need help to break the cycle.

Here's how you do it:

1. Document, Document, Document
    Identify the onset. Was there a triggering event? What was it? When did it occur? I'm lucky in that my latest trigger came in the form of an email, so I can go back and see exactly when I got the news.
    How has your sleep been? As a bipolar patient, you should be prepared to answer this question for any of your professionals at any time because it can be such a tremendous help in diagnosing a manic, depressive, or mixed episode.
    What (other) symptoms have you had? Just write down which symptoms you have and let the psychiatric professional sort out what it means. You can use this list (modified from the National Institute of Mental Health).
    - Feeling very up, high, elated, extremely irritable,

hypersensitive, or angry
- Feeling jumpy or wired, more active than usual
- Having a decreased need for sleep
- Having trouble falling asleep, waking up too early, or sleeping too much
- Talking as though you can't get the words out fast enough ("pressured speech")
- Talking very slowly, feeling unable to find anything to say, or forgetting a lot
- Racing thoughts ("flight of ideas")
- Having trouble concentrating or making decisions
- Feeling able to do many things at once without getting tired
- Feeling unusually important, talented, or powerful
- Feeling very down, sad, or anxious
- Feeling slowed down or unable to sit still
- Feeling unable to do even simple things
- Having an excessive appetite for food, drinking, sex, spending, or other pleasurable activities
- Having a lack of interest in almost all activities
- Feeling hopeless or worthless or thinking about death or suicide

2. **Contact Your Therapist for a Second Opinion.** Let your therapist know what's going on. Share your documentation with them. If they feel your concerns are valid, definitely proceed to the

next step.

3. **Look Into Getting Your Meds Adjusted.** Contact your psychiatric professional and let them know that you think you're having an episode and that you think you may need your meds adjusted. If you're not sure if you're having an episode, but something is definitely "off", let them know what is "off", so they can prioritize you on their schedule. If you cannot get into to see your psychiatric professional or you are in crisis, skip to step 5.

4. **Explore Outpatient Treatment.** This is where you attend inpatient-type therapy without being admitted for 24/7 observation. Contact your psychiatric professional or health insurance company or provider to see if this is a good option for you.

5. **Embrace Inpatient Treatment.** Yes, I know I have said the goal is to avoid hospitalization, but sometimes it is the best option. If you have tried everything else, then it is the only option. It's much better for you to go off the rails in a controlled environment than to do it on your own, where you could hurt yourself or someone else. It's easier on everyone if you go voluntarily, including you.

If you choose to go in, then you are more likely to be able to choose when to leave. When everything spirals out of control, just knowing that you have any kind of power makes a huge difference in your state of mind. It also means you have accountability and an investment in your mental health. It means you know you need help and that you are more likely to accept it. You may improve faster, and that could mean a shorter stay.

Also, know this. All facilities/hospitals are not the same. They do not screen and train their employees the same. They do not offer the same level of support and care. Personally, I would rather go to one that has a committed staff of folks with master's degrees than one with a reputation for abuse. Figure out which is which in your area by talking with multiple people (like psychiatric professionals and patients) so you have a plan for where to go and are not scrambling if you do need this level of care.

Whichever route you need to go, know this: one day when you have almost given up completely, you'll see a glimmer of light in your world of darkness. You will believe it's a mirage, but it's there. If you focus on it, it will grow. Eventually, the glimmer will get big enough to provide light in your darkness. It will give you the opportunity to view things from a new perspective. Try it. One day there may be more light than there is darkness. The depression may not be over, but it is the perfect time to breathe a sigh of relief because now you know there is hope after all.

Chapter 9

The Best and Worst of Times

Sometimes you may need hospitalization. I've come to accept that I do. If you're suicidal and you have a plan that you're ready to act on, then throw your medications in a bag, and get yourself to an ER pronto. Don't worry about the cat, the dog, or the plants. Right now, your life is in jeopardy, and you need to take it seriously. Odds are, if you go in when you first need to, you'll be out in three to five days instead of a few weeks.

I live in the United States, so I'm writing this based on my experience with US health care, specifically privatized US health care. I've had a total of four hospitalizations as of the date I'm writing this. I'm going to tell you about each of them and tell you how to make a plan for your own hospitalizations, should you need one.

My first hospitalization was during my divorce when I was staying in the guest room at my then-husband's and my house. I woke up at 2 a.m. crying and became suicidal by 4. At 5:30 I got up and got dressed. At 6, I took the dog to him and told him I needed to go to the ER and why. He didn't take my concerns seriously; I went anyway. They "Baker Acted" me, which is slang in Florida for putting you on an involuntary seventy-two-hour hold for observation. (Baker Act is the name of the law there that allows them to protect you from yourself. It has a different name in every state.) I was given paper scrubs, and they took everything except my phone. I was sedated and spent most of the day sleeping in a bed in the ER. Late that afternoon, I was informed that a bed had opened up at a facility in the area, and they would be transporting me there by ambulance.

The facility, it turned out, was wonderful. It was a combination mental health and substance abuse inpatient treatment center divided into men's and women's units. We were supervised 24/7. All of the activity leaders had a master's degree or higher—and the activities were fabulous. Amazing art therapy, group therapy, and coping skills. I still remember how we had to draw ourselves as a tree and explain it to the group. We submitted morning and evening reports to our psychiatrists. It was here that I learned how severe my anxiety truly was. As a result, they were able to start me on a higher dose of anxiety medication than they would've been able to do in an outpatient setting. It was life changing. Those were some of the pros.

The cons? (And let me say, some of these were pros at the time.) I spent the first three days in the same tear-stained paper scrubs because I hadn't packed any clothes. I spent the whole first day sobbing, but so did everyone else who came to the unit. You eat what they give you when they give it to you, or you don't eat. You have access to limited personal hygiene products: don't bring your toothbrush, toothpaste, or, in some cases, deodorant because they won't let you have them. Say goodbye to your shampoo and soap, too—they give you combo shampoo and body wash. No makeup. No mirrors to put it on with. No sharp edges. No plastic bags. Your toilet paper holder is a round hole in the wall. All the fixtures are designed for your safety. Oh, and I had a homicidal roommate, but we got along pretty well.

My total length of stay was four days. All in all? It was wonderful. I wouldn't change a thing.

I don't remember what triggered my second hospitalization, but I was separated from my husband, in Alabama, and hadn't researched facilities. I was too ignorant to know what great luck I'd had the first time around. Therefore, I didn't know that I needed to do my homework. I went to the ER at my closest hospital, and they admitted me to their psych ward. This time I had expectations. If only I had known how high the bar had been set.

No homicidal roommate this time. In fact, my roommate was totally cool. The staff, however, was a different story. A nurse got into an argument with my roommate and threatened to withhold her meds. When we did "art therapy," there was no purpose to it. I should know. I asked. They were supposed to check our vitals twice a day and didn't do it. I think it was on my third day there that my roommate called the posted hotline to report the staff to the directors. They quickly lined us up to check our vitals. I remember that someone's blood pressure was out of acceptable range, and they had the person sit in a chair and do breathing exercises so they could come back to them. They were busted, and they knew it. I tell everyone I know never to go there.

During my third hospitalization, I never left the ER. I spent three days in a specialized psych section of the emergency room, and the nurses took such good care of me that I improved to the point that they did not need to admit me. I saw psychiatrists, social workers, and caseworkers. This facility had their act together. I had heard that they were the best in town, and that's why I went there. They did not disappoint. One of the nurses had a semicolon tattooed on the inside of her wrist for suicide prevention. I was so inspired by her that I got one just like it the night I got out.

My fourth hospitalization, they almost didn't admit me, but they did and were wonderful. It was as great a facility as my first hospitalization, though in different ways. It was a coed (men and women) unit set up for roommates that were used as singles, so there was only one person in each room. It was for patients aged 18 and up. (Younger people were kept in a separate unit.) It was strictly mental health. We did physical exercises (nothing strenuous) and worked on coping tools. Everyone who worked there was well-trained, and they operated by the book and were genuinely concerned about our well-being. We had a case manager who coordinated with someone on the outside to make sure we were successful in coming home, even in cases like mine where we lived alone or for another woman who lived out of town.

If you've never been hospitalized, it will be a shock. You are going there to focus on yourself and your healing. If you want Club Med, you will not heal there as quickly as you will in a hospital or crisis center setting.

Here's what you need to know about hospitalization:

- I always felt safe from everyone, including myself, which I didn't on the outside at the time.

- Your intake may be a shock. They go through all of your stuff. All of it. Try to remember that they're just doing their jobs. You'll get it back.

- You won't have your cell phone, but you may have access to a phone free of charge. That access is limited. Take a written list of numbers (two or three people at the most) that you want to contact.

- You can have your own clothes, with a few exceptions, such as those with strings and laces, or you may have to "earn" the privilege of wearing your own clothes instead of scrubs.

- There may be a television (with cable channels) in the common room(s) for your viewing. Please note that access may be limited. This is for your protection.

- You will be asked to cooperate (take medication and participate in group and individual activities). You will have a choice as to whether or not to do these things. Your willingness and ability to participate in your own healing is an indicator of how much you need to be there and will determine, to some extent, how long they keep you.

- You will be on a predetermined schedule.

- You may have to earn some privileges.

- People do everything from sleeping to crying to walking the halls to playing cards to reading to coloring to watching TV to pass the time.

If someone you care about has been hospitalized,

they may not even tell you. If they do, it means they trust you not to treat them like a different person or a leper because they were hospitalized. So, honor that trust. Treat them like the person they are. You'll both be better for it.

Chapter 10

The Abyss

The first time I tried to kill myself, I was thirteen years old. I hated school. I hated my life. Forget being discouraged to express myself, I was encouraged not to *be* myself.

My family wanted me to be who they wanted. They gave me clothes that *they* wanted me to like. They wanted my friends to be only the ones that *they* approved of. Incidentally, this continued through my wedding, where my mother refused to invite not only my husband's college roommate but also one of our closest friends. Thankfully, they crashed the wedding. I was twenty-five. You can imagine how extreme the situation was in junior high school.

Classmates were mean in the way kids are at thirteen. I was teased—not incessantly but persistently. There was no such thing as bullying awareness then. I worked to fit in with a group of outcasts, but that's hard when you aren't allowed to go anywhere outside of school with them.

I entered an academic program for "gifted" students. All of us made easy targets, ridiculed because we were smart. The tougher classes translated to lots of homework. I got on a schedule where I would watch television in my bedroom until about 11:00 p.m. Then I would start my homework. I would go to sleep between 3:00 and 5:00 a.m., get up at 6:30, then sleep through as much of school as possible. I was an expert at escapism from my undiagnosed mixed state: when I was upset, I would sleep. It was a quick and easy way to take a break from reality, especially when I had stayed up most of the night. I'd come home from school, have a fight with the family, and go pass out on my bed until dinner.

For understandable reasons, and by that, I mean I can trace the origins of the thoughts to something that made some sense in its context one or two generations prior to this, my parents were concerned about appearances. This meant I was not allowed to discuss any "family problems" outside of the family, and hell would rain down on me in the form of multiple tempers if I violated this unspoken rule. How did I learn this? Well, since the rule was unspoken, I was unaware of it until I was the target of said fiery tempers. This keeping of secrets included not only friends but also the school guidance counselor. That's right. I got in trouble with my parents for turning to the one authority figure I was supposed to reach out to. The counselor's husband worked at the same company as my dad. My parents were too busy worrying about what everyone thought of them and me to notice that I was becoming suicidal.

They thought they were helping. Really, they did. My mother still believes that she didn't do enough: "I tried so hard to make you normal." But telling someone with low self-esteem that the world does not revolve around them and that if they remain on their current path, then they will become a "burden on society" is not an approved treatment for depression. That's how I came to the decision to kill myself.

A bathroom adjoined my bedroom upstairs in our house. Frosted glass globes covered the bulbs that lit my vanity. Except one. It had been missing when we moved into the house, and we had not bothered to track down a matching replacement. Thin glass covered the filament in the exposed bulb. It was a Sunday afternoon. I climbed on the counter and unscrewed the bulb from the socket. I stood over my sink, holding the metal in my hand, almost, *almost* ready to smash it in the sink and cut my wrists. I don't know why it mattered not to make a mess with the glass. Was I worried about hurting myself or being neat? Obviously, I had not fully thought this through.

While I was staring at the object, building up my nerve to crack it like an egg on the edge of the sink, I heard my father coming upstairs. As quickly and quietly as one can toss aside a light bulb without shattering it, which is not very, I did so and moved to the bed. I tried to act casually. He was kind and caring, as both my parents frequently were when his and mom's tempers did not dictate their actions. It was completely fucked up. The very people who were driving me to kill myself managed to interrupt my first meager attempt.

I don't remember what he said, what we talked about, but when he left, I returned to the bathroom and screwed the light bulb back in the socket.

Be Prepared for Suicidal Thoughts

You have bipolar disorder. You have a chemical imbalance in your brain, which makes you predisposed to going off the rails. All it takes is one little thing, and your mind can tumble over the edge of sanity into an abyss where you can't see the bottom, and the light drifts farther and farther away until you can't tell which way is up. *That is not your fault.* I repeat, *that is not your fault.*

However, it *is* your responsibility to do your best to let people know you need help. If you don't signal that you're drowning, no one will know you need a life preserver. Here is what to do: Call your doctor. Call your therapist. Drive to a doctor's office or hospital. You are in a medical crisis and need to be seen as surely as if you broke your arm.

I had been living in Florida for a year when I had a meltdown at work and tried to quit my job. We had an EAP, and my boss begged me to see a counselor before I quit. She even called the counselor for me. On my first visit, the counselor told me that she thought I might have bipolar, and I should follow up with my doctor. I planned to go the following Wednesday when it was convenient.

Episodes don't care about your schedule and what is convenient for you. On Tuesday, I was in a full day of classes in graduate school when suddenly, one of the other students contradicted something I said. I took it personally and became so upset I had to leave class. A friend who came to check on me found me sobbing in my car. I couldn't stop crying. She didn't know what to do. That was one of those friendships that became perpetually awkward after that moment. I wasn't invited to her wedding.

I used my cell phone to call my new counselor. I don't remember if I caught her in between patients or if she called me back. She stayed on the phone with me until I was calm enough to drive and then until I arrived at my doctor's office. Diagnosis confirmed and pill samples in hand, I was terrified, but I had an immense sense of relief.

It wasn't me.

It wasn't my fault that I had wanted a big truck to hit my car and kill me to stop the misery.

It wasn't that I couldn't control my emotions or behavior because I wasn't trying hard enough.

It's not you.

It's not your fault that you want to die.

It's not because you're not good enough or strong enough or tall enough or just enough.

You're sick, just like I am.

Is it a person's fault if they have asthma? It's not your fault you have bipolar disorder. Like asthma, it isn't something you can catch. If you're in crisis, it's no different than having an asthma attack. Both can kill you if you don't get medical help and get it fast. If you are suicidal, you are having an episode and need to see your doctor as soon as possible. If their office is closed because it's before hours or after hours or on a weekend or because it's International Chocolate Day, then go to an emergency room. If you can't drive, get someone to take you. If you can't find anyone you trust to drive you, then call 911. They will not judge you. I should have called 911 when I fell, got a concussion, dislocated my shoulder, broke it in three places, and tore a tendon in my knee and a ligament in my ankle. It took me 15 minutes to crawl to the phone. I didn't call 911 because I was embarrassed that I was still in my pajamas at 1:00 in the afternoon. I called a friend who talked me into thinking that I was fine; she failed to tell me she was so depressed that she couldn't get out of bed and that I should call someone else. Like 911.

Oh, but I'm not dressed. I haven't showered or brushed my teeth. And how will they get in? I can't leave the bed to go unlock the door.

You may think these irrational thoughts just like I did when I had a concussion. Firemen have seen scarier things than you in your pajamas. EMTs have seen creepier things than you naked. And as far as getting to you? It's their job to get to places where people need help. If they have "the jaws of life" to pry people out of cars that have been turned into sardine cans, what makes you think they can't get you out of your house or apartment? Tell them you need them, and they will take it from there. All you have to do is do nothing until they arrive. So count floor tiles, make patterns in the carpet, twiddle your thumbs, or sing songs from "Mary Poppins." You probably won't even have to decide what to do because the 911 operators are trained for situations like this and, just like in any other emergency, will keep you on the phone until the paramedics are in the room with you. When they knock on your door, answer it if you can. If not, let them come in and get you.

I'm not against suicide hotlines. I have called them before; they were helpful. That was before I had been diagnosed and understood the nature of this illness. *You need to see a physician pronto.* There are no asthma hotlines to call when you are having an attack. You are having the psychiatric equivalent of an asthma attack. You need a doctor to give you drugs to get better. Fast. Or really bad things could happen. Like you might actually do yourself physical harm, and that would suck.

I should know. My mother-in-law attempted to overdose twelve states away around midnight because her husband asked for a divorce. She is bipolar, though it was a closely guarded secret from pretty much everyone except her. We knew something was off—that's kind of obvious when your husband's earliest memories are of his mom's suicide attempts. That's right, plural. She didn't share her diagnosis with me until ten years after this event when I shared mine with her.

Anyway, my husband and I arrived home from a lovely date on a Friday evening and went to bed at 11:30 p.m. It was early July, and we had been married ten months. At midnight the phone rang, and my mother-in-law slurred that she wanted us to have the China cabinet. Then my husband was on the phone with her, and I was on the phone with 911 in another part of the country trying to explain where she lived—because we had been there but I couldn't find the address because when you get woken up at midnight by someone who has downed every pill in their house including Tylenol and chased it with a liter of vodka (I'm speaking literally here), that's the kind of stuff that goes wrong. They found her. They saved her. We were up all night and on a 7 a.m. flight Saturday morning. She was in ICU for days as the doctors assessed her psychiatric state as well as organ damage, including her heart, brain, liver, and kidneys.

I was in the hospital room when she was screaming for a bedpan, mortified that her bowels were releasing yet still delirious from the toxins in her system. I picked up the little pieces of plastic they peel off when they attach the electrodes to your chest so they can monitor your heart rate from where the paramedics left them on the living room floor. I cleaned the lace curtains of the semi-dissolved pills they were spattered with from when her body projectile vomited the contents of her stomach against her will. I stood by my husband as he spoke with doctors. We made plans. No, she could not be left alone.

We took her into our house for two weeks then and another four weeks when she became suicidal again two months later. The second time I almost had a nervous breakdown. All of this happened years before my diagnosis. I would work late, then come home and lock myself in the bathroom. The Saturday after she finally left, I woke up, started crying, and couldn't stop. My husband did not scare easily, but he didn't know what to do when I couldn't stop. That was it. She was not allowed to move in with us again, though she asked for years. We wouldn't sacrifice my mental health for hers.

It's not that she's not a nice person. She's perfectly lovely *when she is on her meds*. But she lies to her doctors. She lies to us. She lies to everyone. Which means she won't let them help her.

Unless that changes, there's no happy ending for her.

But there can be for you and me. Be honest with your doctors. Take your medications. Find a way to do therapy, even if you're just working through self-help books at home. There will still be good days and bad, including some really rough moments. Our moods swing. That's what they do. And if one day, in one moment, you find yourself in a really bad place, please know it can get better if only you can get to a doctor. If nothing else, they can knock you out safely for a while.

I drove myself to an emergency room because I seriously considered downing a bottle of pills to check out permanently. I had moved and couldn't contact my old psychiatrist because he was out on medical leave. I knew the stress of the move and my list of 25+ things to do had finally triggered an episode. When I told my husband that I needed to go to the ER, he said, "Sit down. Let's talk about this." I responded with, "Protocol says..." He didn't ask me to finish the sentence. I walked out of the room, waited to see if I could calm down, then drove myself to the ER.

Now, I could call an Uber or a Lyft. I could also have called a taxi or asked a friend or family member to drive me. The point is, I knew I needed help, and I got it.

For further understanding, please get "This Is How" by Augusten Burroughs and read the chapter titled "How to End Your Life." There is always a better option than killing yourself. Augusten explains how he did exactly that, so it can be done.

Chapter 11

Triggers

You know to lower your HDLs from your doctor. I'm here to tell you to lower your TTL—your Trigger Tolerance Level. This is much easier said than done, especially if you're a people pleaser or have dominant personalities in your life that are used to using you as a doormat. It takes practice. It also gets easier with practice because you reap the benefits, and that will motivate you.

Therapy will be immensely helpful to you with this. You want a therapist that will help you identify and set boundaries with your triggers.

This can essentially be distilled into three steps:

1. Identify the trigger. Ask your therapist, make notes, keep a log—whatever works for you.
2. Set a boundary. If it works, you're done. If not, proceed to the next step.

3. Set a stricter boundary. If this still doesn't work, continue with this until you get to an acceptable place, which may mean going to extremes.

You don't need to be an asshole about any of it. You can be polite and stand firm. You don't need to feel guilty, either. In fact, there are some communities where taking care of yourself is considered and referred to as "The Prime Directive."

In my case, my parents (both of them—separately and together) were huge triggers for me. My mother used to introduce me to her friends and then say, "I tried so hard to make her normal," right in front of me. Dad threatened to block me on Facebook over politics because of something he misinterpreted. I got in trouble with both of them for going for mental/emotional help from the junior high school counselor —heaven forbid anyone knew our secrets.

If your partner or parent is not making your mental health a priority, that's considered neglect. If they are choosing to keep you from getting the help you need for personal gain or to avoid personal loss—be that income, friends, reputation, whatever—that is abuse.

At the age of 52, my parents still wanted me to check in every morning with a phone call. We live in the same city, and I work from home, writing on a computer. I asked them for some simple things: stop trying to change me, don't discuss our vastly different politics with me, don't make fun of me, etc. They didn't do this. I went to daily "proof of life" texts to them and my sister and weekly phone calls, where we mostly discussed recipes. Again and again, they violated my boundaries, calling and upsetting me unnecessarily. Things escalated. Before it was over, I informed them that the daily group texts would be stopping, and my boyfriend would let them know if there was a problem. My sister replied, "Fuck off, sister dear." My parents did not respond at all.

I've been no contact with my parents since then. Did I grieve? Yes. I grieved for the parents I should have had and the positive aspects of the relationships. I have also stopped being triggered almost daily, greatly reduced my anxiety attacks, rarely have to take my as-needed anxiety meds during the day, and have improved my self-esteem and overall quality of life beyond measure.

Is it hard? Yes. Many people don't understand. A lot of the time, they blame me and my bipolar disorder, which sucks. I have over 1,000 hours of therapy under my belt and made none of these decisions in a vacuum. People who really know me know that I wouldn't do this lightly. People who know my parents are confused because they're perfectly nice to everyone else. They can't imagine them behaving any other way. It's also created some problems with my cousin, who originally asked to be left out of this business but then started sharing her opinions with me after spending some time with my parents. She is no longer a "safe zone" for me, and I am making changes, so I don't get blindsided by her in social situations.

Is it harder than staying in contact with them and getting triggered all the time? Absolutely not.

I had to stop the bleeding so I could heal. My sister and I are negotiating boundaries, as she feels the need for me to reconcile with our parents. That's not going to happen. Do I have some hard decisions ahead of me? Yes. I know that. I will handle them with the help of my therapist, partner, and chosen family. My parents are 80+ years old. Will I attend their funerals? I don't know. I will burn that bridge when I get to it.

For now, I have more peace than I have ever had, and that is priceless. Can I live with my decision if I don't wake up tomorrow? You bet I can.

I'm in an extreme situation that called for extreme measures after two decades of therapy. Your situation will be different from mine. You will need to look at different things. Or maybe the same. I only know my experience.

A funny thing happens when you lower your TTL: your CTL (Crap Tolerance Level) goes down as well. You're just much less willing to put up with anyone's crap. This happens because your self-esteem and self-respect have increased if you are doing this in a healthy way. You begin to set more and more healthy boundaries because it's much easier once you learn how to do it.

The more you practice, the better you get, and it has the most wonderful effect snowball effect. Your relationships can become almost drama-free to the point where it's just the regular ups and downs of life. And that's a beautiful thing.

Chapter 12

A Different Approach

Many people think this is New Age mumbo jumbo. If you're one of them, that's fine. You can skip this section. If you're open to positive visualization as a potential tool for your arsenal, read on.

The law of attraction can be simply stated in a number of ways:

Like attracts like, or

Thoughts become things, or

Man becomes what he thinks about.

Like the law of gravity, this works whether you believe in it or not. You can imagine how challenging it is to make this work for you when you often do not have control over your own thoughts. There are numerous books, CDs, and videos on the market explaining the law of attraction in great detail. (You can find a list of a few of these in Recommended Reading and Exercises.)

So how does this work? While I'm no quantum physicist, I can tell you it's based on energy. The step-by-step instructions I received on this were as follows:

Ask.
Believe.
Receive.

Sounds simple enough, right? Not if you have bipolar disorder.

Experts on the Law of Attraction, such as Abraham-Hicks and contributors to *The Secret*, make a point to let you know that you have chosen to be where you are. That's truly a bitter pill to swallow when you can be a hostage of your moods. This is one of the many reasons why you need to spend more time taking control of your life.

One easy way to start doing this is to listen to your inner voice and how it fits with your behavior. For example, if you are habitually late, your inner voice may say things like, "I'm late," or "I'm going to be late." Your body and your mind believe that you're behind schedule. You feel like you're running late. Adrenalin kicks in. Your heart rate and blood pressure increase. Your breathing becomes shallow. Then your mind kicks in. Your inner voice starts adding things like, "Why can't you ever get anywhere on time?" and "Do you realize how disrespectful you are?" This only makes the situation worse. Your behavior is eroding your self-esteem. You've entered a negative cycle.

What if instead of telling yourself, "I'm late," you tell yourself, "I'm early"? Try it right now. Think about your next appointment and tell yourself, "I'm early." How does it make you feel? Are you relaxed? Sit with it for a minute or two. How is your breathing? Is it rapid, or is it relatively slow? If you physically feel better, then you know the self-talk is working. By focusing on this mindset before appointments, your inner voice can begin to impact your behavior in a positive way. What you speak will come to pass. You become what you think, and if you think you're early, then you eventually will be. Now you're in control. You've stopped beating yourself up because you have no reason to do so. You have broken the cycle.

This may not seem like a big deal. You've changed one thing, and you're still bipolar. Ten minutes from now, you may be depressed again. How does this matter?

You have a new skill. You have a new awareness. You know how to pay attention to your inner voice. That is a big deal.

As you implement your self-talk, there are a few important things to remember. Words matter. You'll notice that in the example, you don't say, "I will not be late." In this sentence, the focus is still on the word "late." Therefore, the phrasing and corresponding mindset can still contribute to the behavior of being late. Instead, you should replace the negative word with its opposite, a positive one. In this case, the opposite of "late" is "early." You replace the thought "I'm late" with "I'm early." "Late," which has a negative connotation, has been replaced with a word that creates positive feelings. You must replace negative with positive to experience the shift.

I see this whole process as similar to the visualization that professional athletes do. It helped me reframe what I was already working on. That's why I'm sharing. Take it or leave it, whatever works for you. If you'd like to explore a depression-friendly approach, I recommend "Ask and It Is Given" by Esther and Jerry Hicks.[9] I prefer to use a paperback copy for reference. They have specific exercises called processes to help you feel better, but here is the awesome part: they have a spectrum of twenty-two emotions ranging from joy to despair that correspond to the processes. It also tells you when to use them.

For example, "Process #22: Moving Up the Emotional Scale" is suggested for a depressive episode or when you have been diagnosed with a "frightening illness" (ahem, that's you). On the scale of emotions, it's appropriate if you fall between "(17) Anger" and "(22) Fear/Grief/Depression/Despair/Powerlessness."[10] If you're in a great mood or anywhere in between, they have processes for those, too.

Maybe it can help you.

Chapter 13

Maintenance

One day, you should reach the point where your medications are in balance. You will be able to deal with daily stress without falling apart. You can get out of bed yet not stay up all night. You don't scream at people over the smallest things. You don't burst into tears for no reason. You can see your therapist every two to four weeks without freaking out in between. You can go six months at a time without seeing your doctor.

This is, in a word, awesome. I don't mean that in the "cool" sense of the word, which it definitely is. I mean it in the sense that you and those close to you are filled with awe at how far you have come in dealing with your bipolar disorder. You will be amazed at how good it feels to have those mood swings relatively controlled. At how good it feels not to have to apologize for being irrational or lashing out in anger.

At how good it feels to be on cruise control without constantly being on guard about what is going on with your episodes.

When you reach a balanced state (and this is relative), you want to maintain it for as long as possible. You've worked really hard to get here. It's much easier to *stay* here. You do that by:

- Taking your medication as directed.

- Taking your medication as directed.

- Taking your medication as directed.

- Keeping scheduled appointments with your psychiatrist, whether that is every two weeks or every six months.

- Keeping weekly, biweekly, or monthly appointments with your therapist. This should be determined by how stable you are and by your finances.

- Working between appointments to make progress.

- Keeping a consistent schedule, including when you go to bed and when you get up. Note: there are great apps and wristbands for tracking your sleep. You can watch the captured information to observe if you are trending toward mania or depression. You can also share the results with your doctor and therapist.

- Do your self-care, whatever that is. It must be paid like taxes. You are the only one who can choose when to do it. However, if you choose not to do it, the bill will come due and probably not in a nice way.

This is not rocket science. You can do this. The only reason I was able to finish this book right was because I was stable and in a maintenance phase. It can happen for you, too. It takes a lot of work, but it is so worth it.

Always remember you feel better *because you are taking your meds.* If you decide that because you feel better, you can stop taking your medication, I will almost guarantee you that you will have a major episode in a matter of days as the drugs taper off in your system. Psychiatric professionals will tell you this. Therapists will tell you this. People who have bipolar friends and family members will tell you this.

You are not the exception. You are not special. I am begging you to listen to me. This is how people with bipolar disorder get jacked up eight ways from Sunday. This is how they wind up on the news because an airplane had to make an emergency landing because someone with bipolar disorder who was off their meds freaked out in the middle of their flight. Do not be that person.

Be the reasonable person who doesn't fly off the handle. Be the healthy person who makes thoughtful decisions in their own best interest. Be the best possible version of you. Then everyone is happy.

If you even *think* about going off your meds, come back and read this again. Then read the section on medication. Then read this one more time.

Chapter 14

The Workplace

I came out at work right after my two-year anniversary at my job in November 2023.

Yes, you read that right. I came out to our Diversity, Equity, and Inclusion (DEI) Committee and spilled my guts for the sake of getting mental health on the company radar.

I'm a top performer (not perfect, mind you) on an awesome team with terrific stats. I'm stable at work the vast majority of the time, and folks had no idea what I was dealing with. I only came out at that level to my boss, her boss (his boss was on the DEI Committee), and my two colleagues. As we roll it out to the rest of the company, I'm going to share a little bit less with my larger department (my boss's boss's group of 20-25 employees) and then even less with the company at large (40,000 employees), for which they've asked me to make a video with the aid of our internal professionals.

Do I recommend coming out at work like I did? Absolutely not. There's still too much of a stigma associated with bipolar disorder. I'm the exception, not the rule, in this case.

If You Have Bipolar and Are Working

How should you handle work when you have bipolar disorder?

First things first. You were hired to do a job. Do it. Do it well, if you can. That's the baseline.

But what if you can't? It's time for a hard look at yourself and what you're capable of doing (and not doing) and, more importantly, why. Is it because you're not qualified? Or are you qualified, but bipolar disorder is interfering with your ability to do the job?

If that's the case, are you doing everything you can to manage your bipolar disorder? For example, can your medication be adjusted? Does it need to be for you to be effective at work? Are you applying yourself in therapy? Have you enlisted your therapist's help in problem-solving the situation(s)?

Can you do the job with some accommodation? What kind? Are they appropriate for your position, or are you better suited for another position?

While bipolar disorder is classified as a disability under the Americans with Disabilities Act (ADA), that doesn't guarantee you unlimited protections for any job you want. Nothing does.

Quite honestly, the hardest part of any job is working with people, whether that's your boss, direct reports, colleagues, internal customers, external customers, vendors, or clients—and I'm sure I've missed a few. I have yet to encounter a job that does not involve working with people in some capacity. It requires nuanced skills that I am still working to master after two-plus decades of therapy. I still have to work really, really hard at it. And I'm a likable person. I just can't be consistent because I have bipolar. No matter how hard I try. And I have to be responsible for my actions, just like you do, which sucks. That said, in my reviews, I've told my boss what my limitations are —and that it's not that I'm not working on them. My weaknesses are my weaknesses. I try to improve and will keep trying.

The fact is, no one is one hundred percent consistent. We just stand out more because we're less consistent than average, and when we swing, we swing a little farther. As a result, when we're great, we're really awesome. And when we're not, well, we're not. Either way, it's noticeable.

Sometimes, even when we think we're doing the right thing and it seems like all systems are "go," everything can go to hell in a handbasket in a hot minute because of something we didn't know about. Because of something we couldn't have known about. We can be blindsided by a perfect storm. Then comes the criticism, constructive or otherwise. The best advice I can give for those times is just to try to figure out how not to make it any worse. That's usually by shutting up and listening. Three decades in corporate America, sales, and teaching, and that's what I have for you.

After you listen, you'll decide about how to weigh what was said to you. Was it accurate? Was it off-base? You may know while you're listening, or it may take some time for you to digest. Either way, I try to maintain my composure and say, "Thank you." It doesn't matter if they were so far off base that I completely disassociated. That's what I was trained to do. Notice I'm not saying for *you* to do that. Honestly, I don't know *how* I have been able to do it. I don't recommend the Johnny Paycheck "Take This Job and Shove It" approach. You can go through an awful lot of jobs that way.

The important thing is for you to find a way to be yourself without allowing your bipolar disorder to run roughshod and let you fly off the handle and ultimately shoot yourself in the foot without your permission. I strongly recommend working with your therapist on this if you have a temper. I'm not an employment lawyer. I don't even play one on TV.

I did a deep dive into some basic skills that they evaluate when looking at mental disabilities, and I am sorely lacking in some of them. That said, I try to make up for my shortcomings by excelling in other areas to bring value to my company. I also try to exhibit a positive attitude as much as possible.

It's all working together, at least right now. But that's all any of us really has, isn't it?

Work-Related Symptoms

In doing research for this book, I had a horrendous wake-up call. I discovered that I have deficits in not just two (as I thought) but in all four categories—as my therapist pointed out—of work-related symptoms as described by the Social Security Administration:

> "**Understand, remember, or apply information**. This area of mental functioning refers to the abilities to learn, recall, and use information to perform work activities. Examples include: understanding and learning terms, instructions, procedures; following one- or two-step oral instructions to carry out a task; describing work activity to someone else; asking and answering questions and providing explanations; recognizing a mistake and correcting it; identifying and solving problems; sequencing multi-step activities; and using reason and judgment to make work-related decisions. These examples illustrate the nature of this area of mental functioning.
>
> "**Interact with others**. This area of mental functioning refers to the abilities to relate to and work with supervisors, co-workers, and the public.

Examples include: cooperating with others; asking for help when needed; handling conflicts with others; stating own point of view; initiating or sustaining conversation; understanding and responding to social cues (physical, verbal, emotional); responding to requests, suggestions, criticism, correction, and challenges; and keeping social interactions free of excessive irritability, sensitivity, argumentativeness, or suspiciousness. These examples illustrate the nature of this area of mental functioning.

"**Concentrate, persist, or maintain pace.** This area of mental functioning refers to the abilities to focus attention on work activities and stay on task at a sustained rate. Examples include: initiating and performing a task that you understand and know how to do; working at an appropriate and consistent pace; completing tasks in a timely manner; ignoring or avoiding distractions while working; changing activities or work settings without being disruptive; working close to or with others without interrupting or distracting them; sustaining an ordinary routine and regular attendance at work; and working a full day without needing more than the allotted number or length of rest periods during the day. These examples illustrate the nature of this area of mental functioning.

"**Adapt or manage oneself.** This area of mental functioning refers to the abilities to regulate emotions, control behavior, and maintain well-being in a work setting. Examples include: responding to demands; adapting to changes; managing your psychologically based symptoms; distinguishing between acceptable and unacceptable work performance; setting realistic goals; making plans for yourself independently of others; maintaining personal hygiene and attire appropriate to a work setting; and being aware of normal hazards and taking appropriate precautions. These examples illustrate the nature of this area of mental functioning."[11]

This has been devastating to me for a number of reasons. I've shed a gallon of tears this week, and I haven't cried in months.

First, I've been evaluated against these skills and had my deficits held against me. That doesn't seem fair to me, any more than it would be fair to hold it against someone who had an MS flare-up for not stocking shelves while they were in a wheelchair or on a cane. I'm figuring out how to handle that, both personally and professionally. I'm going to advocate for myself and others, as is my nature, but will have to do so very carefully. After all, I don't want to talk myself out of a job I love.

Second, if I'd received help earlier, I might have

developed better skills by now. Oh well. That's water under the bridge. I'm already no contact with my family to protect myself from their unhealthy words and behaviors, which triggered me almost daily. They can't hurt me anymore. Now I've got something more to work on.

Third, I'm saying goodbye to my dream of being in management in corporate America, at least for now. I don't have the skills to do it well. I require too much supervision. Sometimes reality sucks.

Fourth, I have the unhealthy desire to apologize to a bunch of people at work for having these deficits, and it's not even my fault. So, no apologies, at least from my camp.

Just where do we go from here? What reasonable accommodations do we need to make for the good of my department and the organization as a whole?

I mean, I'm a total badass at my job, generally speaking. I was the first person in my department to achieve professional certification. I drafted our standard operating procedures (SOPs). I run the software that makes our department tick.

How did I handle it after I processed this mess of emotions?

I met with my boss, a human resources representative, and our ADA Coordinator (all together). I had put together a spreadsheet of all the categories in Google Sheets with my potential deficits highlighted. My boss was only concerned about the ones that related to working with others. The rest were non-issues, so

I unmarked them. I had mitigation plans in place for each item, with the first part of each plan being "Kristi addressing" because ultimately, the burden is on me to improve.

My boss made it clear to HR that I was fully competent at my job and that my performance was not an issue, which was reassuring. She explained that I had never been written up for anything and that I had only had "coachings," which are not negative things at our company. She also said that she was not going to change her behavior, which was fine by me. After all, I wasn't looking for a babysitter. I also took the opportunity to cover accommodations for potential hospitalizations and major medication adjustments in case the need ever arises.

We're all good, and it's on the record now in case anything comes up. I'm covered, and so is my boss. Also, the ADA expert briefed me on FMLA (the Family Medical Leave Act) in case I ever need to activate it.

How should you handle it? That will depend on you, your relationship with your boss, your HR department, and your general work environment. Would this have worked for me in every job I've had? Certainly not. But it worked for me here and now. You've got to "read the room." And if you're not sure, it might not hurt to consult a lawyer, though I recommend taking a partnership approach over an adversarial one, if at all possible.

If You Suspect Someone at Work Has Bipolar Disorder

One in five U.S. adults experience mental illness each year.[12]

Let that sink in. While I don't have the perfect one-size-fits-all answer for this, and I don't think there is one, I'm going to attempt to address it.

Don't bring in a consultant to talk to the person alone. This was done to me, and I kept pushing the meeting back until they ultimately gave me a severance package. My co-workers asked me if I thought I needed to meet with them, and I didn't. Look what happened. I would gauge this as an ineffective solution.

Don't report them to HR and expect someone from HR to handle it alone, especially if they don't know them well or at all. This most likely will be regarded as a hostile action and will not encourage the person to seek treatment. Another ineffective solution.

I will say that you may want to consider one of the above options if the person is a valued employee, and it's a last resort to keep from firing them.

Do seek out guidance from HR and your DEI committee (if you have one).

Do see if a trusted supervisor or colleague is willing to broach the topic with them first.

Do try referring them to a counselor at your EAP (if you have one) and if they trust you. This is ultimately how I was diagnosed at the age of 32, after roughly 16 years in the workplace and 20 years with bipolar.

Chapter 15

Bipolar and What Law?

What the hell does bipolar have to do with the law? More than you'd ever imagine in your worst nightmares. One Friday night in December 2023, I received a letter from the my local Law Enforcement Agency Driver License Division. Back in March of 2023, I had renewed my driver's license and gone in person to their office to upgrade to a Real-ID or "Star ID" so I could fly domestically without my passport. My number just happened to get pulled by a state trooper who took me into an office with a desk. When I gave him my required documents, he noticed my essential tremor, which I've had my entire life, and asked me if I had any health conditions. I replied with my essential tremor, bipolar disorder (because I'm an advocate and don't hide it—how else are we going to break the stigma?), and a few other things, commenting that I didn't have seizures or anything else that affected my driving. Guess what?

Based on research going back to 1965, the most recent of which was conducted in 1998, most with small sample sizes—most involving crashes—the National Highway Transportation and Safety Administration (NHTSA) has flagged bipolar disorder as a risk for driving.[13] In their Advanced Roadside Impaired Driving Enforcement (ARIDE) course, they describe bipolar as "a serious mental illness" Then on the next page they say this. "When an officer encounters or suspects a potentially serious medical condition, he/she should consider involving medical services. DREs [Drug Recognition Experts] are trained to recognize signs of medical impairment."[14]

The Division's Medical Unit informed me that I must sign a release acknowledging a law that I could not sue in civil or criminal court and that I must allow my PCP or psychiatrist (it must be an M.D. or D.O.) to release my detailed medical information to them or they would suspend my driving privileges. Also, if they did not find the medical report "acceptable," they would suspend my driving privileges until they received one that was. All the documents were marked "CONFIDENTIAL " Different states have different regulations. Some, like mine, have medical review boards. Yours may or may not. Check your state's or country's laws if you need to know.

My point is this. If keeping your driving privileges

and, therefore, your independence isn't enough to motivate you to get on and stick with a treatment plan, I don't know what is. Yes, I self-reported, but there are a thousand other scenarios where it could come out, and you didn't self-report. Then what are you going to do?

To answer your first question, yes, I retained an attorney. However, since I couldn't sue over this, all I could do for was comply and hope for the best. Known unknowns included:

- I didn't know the psychiatrist who was going to be completing my forms. He supervises my PNP, and I had only seen her once. The psychiatrist I'd been seeing quit practicing.
- While my lawyer said that it would be hard for the state to override my doctor's recommendations, it's not impossible. I didn't know what would happen after I submitted my forms.

I am fully aware that not everyone has access to the resources I have. *I* haven't always had access to the resources I have now. I have access to lawyers to help me. I live in a major metro area with doctors and specialists. I have insurance and an HSA (Health Savings Account) to pay to have the forms filled out as the Medical Unit requires. I have a supportive company that will give me paid time off (PTO) to deal with all of this.

I hope you care enough about yourself that you're

taking care of yourself because you want to. That way, if you do find yourself in this boat, the folks behind this don't have a leg to stand on in your case, either.

Chapter 16

Hope for the Future

When I read Napoleon Hill's "Think and Grow Rich," one particular passage really spoke to my heart: "...handicaps can be converted into stepping stones on which one may climb towards some worthy goal, unless they are accepted as obstacles and used as alibis."[15]

I had been kidding myself for the last few years before I set this book aside. It hurts to admit this. I thought I was doing "well," really. I didn't have other people telling me that I was not succeeding. I didn't have people at work judging me. All of that was because I wasn't working. I was afraid. My fear of work, specifically my fear of failure at work, caused me to self-sabotage opportunities, interviews, contacts, and negotiations. I didn't even see it.

I had been confused about what I wanted. I wanted to reach out for the approval of others while staying safely tucked away in my hobbies at home. I couldn't do both, and I was too full of fear to make a decision. That's why I kept straddling the fence. I would look for jobs and then fail at getting them. I was a different version of myself, and it wasn't working.

Eventually, my husband asked me, "What do you want to do?" With my life. For a living. In general.

I finally figured it out. I had planned my life pre-diagnosis. I had planned to get married and have children. By that time, they would have been in middle school, and my job would have been to be a mom. Granted, we decided not to have children for a number of reasons before my diagnosis, but knowing how sensitive I am to hormones, I would say there was at least a 90% chance of my having a psychotic break and landing strapped down to a bed in a psychiatric unit before the baby was born. Then who would take care of the child? The larger issue is that I never made a new life plan after I had a life-altering event.

Being diagnosed with bipolar disorder is a life-altering event. Your life is now "pre-diagnosis" and "post-diagnosis." You get to define it. You can make it better. Learn about the symptoms. Pay attention to your thoughts and actions. Learn your triggers. I used to live at least two hours away from my parents, and we wouldn't visit each other for more than three days at a time because they were triggers for me. Always have been. Even with those precautions, I have had episodes at their house and been relegated to spending an extra day in their guest bedroom because I was unable to drive home. Since the summer of 2023, I've been no contact.

Do you know what the difference is? Now I know it is not my fault. It's not that I'm being unreasonable. It's not that I need to toughen up because I'm being overly sensitive. I have a chemical imbalance in my brain. While I still have to deal with the results of having a breakdown, I do not blame myself for the breakdown, especially if I do what I am supposed to do by getting away from or neutralizing the trigger. Though the episode is beyond miserable, the peace I have gained from knowing it is not my fault is priceless.

I no longer beat myself up for things that are not my fault. I live with the consequences, but those consequences no longer include self-flagellation. That has given me a better future.

As far as what I want to do with my life, career-wise, I wanted to finish this book to help other people facing a future with bipolar disorder. If I can save one person from one ounce of pain and frustration by writing and publishing this book, then I have made a positive difference in the world. But that isn't how I want to spend all of my time. It's depressing to cry my way through books about parts of my life that I have already moved through. So I made another goal.

I am a huge fan of romance novels. I have been for many, many years since I picked up a Nora Roberts novel in the middle of a pre-diagnosis breakdown (in front of a new senior coworker on a business trip, of course) when I was in the Kansas City airport looking for something, anything to occupy me so I could make it back to Atlanta without bawling through the flight. It did the trick. Nora's novels have saved my sanity more than once, so of course, I had a two-hour breakdown after I finally met her. That's just how it goes.

So, I read more stories by more authors because I wanted to read. I read them because I loved the stories and the characters. I read because I shared *their* Happy Ever Afters, whether I had one or not. I read enough that I ran across stories that were not so well written. I knew that I could write better than some of them. While I had always sucked at writing fiction, I started a journey to do it anyway. I joined organizations and attended workshops where I learned from experts. I discovered I'm not lousy at writing fiction when I have a clue how to do it. I've practiced and practiced, and it's paid off.

I learned that many editors and agents use Twitter for business purposes through a presentation at a meeting at one of the professional organizations I joined. I pitched to an editor there, and she bought four of my manuscripts right away. I would never have guessed that I could do it, but I am.

My first novel won the award for Best Manuscript Submission at the Atlanta Writers Conference. That's right. The girl who couldn't write a story is now an award-winning author. I didn't see that coming, which is probably why I missed the ceremony. (Oops!)

My future is happening now, and it's better than anything I ever imagined. Let yourself dream. Give yourself permission to ask *what if?* You can do more than you think you can. Unless you are in a manic state, in which case you should consult your doctor before you sign up for medical school to become a brain surgeon or join the Peace Corps and move to Zimbabwe without fully thinking it through.

Chapter 17

Taking Control of Your Destiny

You have bipolar disorder. Bipolar disorder does not have you. You have the ability to choose. To start with, you can choose your attitude. You can accomplish almost anything with a positive attitude. The first person who taught me this secret was a vibrant and happily married family man in his mid-forties. I was twenty-six. As we were Alabama natives, I asked him and his wife where they went to college. The standard answer would typically be Auburn or Alabama. Surprisingly, they explained that they had married just out of high school and didn't attend college.

Big deal, you might say. Lots of people don't go to college. How is that surprising?

We were together on a Lear jet headed for New

York. It was one of two planes owned by our company, a five-hundred million dollar-a-year business. He was the president.

I was shocked, as well as embarrassed for asking the question. It's hard to change the subject suddenly or to wander off when you're one of six people aboard a private plane for seven. As fitting his position, the man spun this awkward situation into a teachable moment by sharing how his attitude had consistently contributed to his success. I'll never forget it.

He told me that a positive attitude was more important than anything. I have lived by that advice ever since. Whenever my attitude has slipped, I have seen incredible differences when I've caught myself and made the shift.

Applied Cognitive Behavioral Therapy

Years later, I was in a job where I was miserable. My ego had taken a blow. I was uncomfortable managing my staff. I thought my boss was a jerk. To top it off, our location was the "redheaded stepchild" of our company. We couldn't do anything right as far as they were concerned. As often happens, most of the management and employees commiserated in daily gripe sessions. The negativity was like black tar seeping into every corner of our workplace. It was suffocating our souls.

One day I remembered what the president of my old company had taught me. I began to consider how

I could implement a positive attitude at work. I knew I wouldn't be a cheerleader, but at least I could stop contributing to the gloom.

I only made two changes to my behavior, and I never would've guessed that they would make such a huge difference. The first thing I did was to implement a technique I'd learned from my yoga instructor. During particularly strenuous poses, our teacher would tell us, "Smile. It makes your body think you like it." So, I smiled. Regardless of whether I felt happy or sad or angry or insulted, I smiled. I may have been gritting my teeth part of the time, but I kept smiling.

My second change required a little bit of strategy. I had to find something to say when people were complaining and expected a comment from me. I had to keep it honest. I also knew that I didn't want to argue against the complaints because so many of them were genuine. In the end, I decided upon a neutral phrase: "You don't say." I learned that this could be interpreted as agreement, surprise, enlightenment, or reinforcement—people could hear what they wanted to hear. This may seem so minor. It was, however, a huge change. I had shifted gears from reverse to neutral. I had made a conscious decision to stop serving as a channel for negativity. It changed my life.

This doesn't mean that I'm always that way. I'm not, at all. I still get pissed off at the world and scream and cry and don't care about eating and want to get drunk and don't want to get out of bed and procrastinate about things I really don't want to do that need doing (like writing about suicide). The difference is that I take time to wallow in my misery, but somehow, some way, in minutes or hours or days or weeks, I pull myself out of it because I know that I'm the only one who can do that for me.

Augusten Burroughs says, "Any damage that's been done, you have to fix yourself because it needs fixing and there is nobody else to do the work."[16] That doesn't mean you don't need help; we need help, like asthmatics need inhalers. You have to reach out for it. After all, my inhaler won't help me if I leave it in my purse.

Truth and Consequences

Life won't be perfect. I have a trail of broken friendships littering my past, collateral damage from my illness. There were those moments at work where I asked my bosses for the sun and the moon and the stars, fully believing that it was possible to make the ridiculous happen, fully convinced that it was a critical necessity, fully delusional in my manic state. You don't get to take those moments back. Neither do the other millions of people who have bipolar disorder and who do some version of the same damn thing. Like the ones who burst out in tears in their boss's office and can't stop crying but are trying to explain that it's "normal" and that the boss might as well be talking to the wall for all the good it's doing, as he or she tries to get you to stop. There's that message again, the one that is the bane of my existence: *You are not trying hard enough.*

I kept the job where I had the delusional request, though I didn't get what I asked for. I lost the job where I cried, and my boss's boss told me I would never work in that industry again, which was a long, horrible story that had little to do with the crying. I couldn't have saved that position no matter what I did, so I moved on and took comfort in the fact that the boss's boss's bosses removed him from his position. And I've never tried to work in that industry again. I moved on. I had nightmares from time to time and would have to take my "in case of emergency break glass" pills, but that's what I have them for. If you need them, your doctor will give them to you, too.

The first anxiety attack I had was about a week after our apartment flooded. It was a different kind of stress because we lived on the thirty-first floor of a high rise. My husband left town for two weeks on business almost immediately after. Some wonderful friends came to help me move our furniture and everything else to a different apartment. But one day, by myself, I cried and was completely falling apart, lying on the hardwood floor of our empty new living room. I called my psychiatrist and left a message with his emergency service. He called me back after about twenty minutes of forever, and I sobbed to him that I needed to know which hospital he wanted me to go to while I could still drive myself. He asked me questions, as good psychiatrists do, then told me he was calling me in some medication. *Oh. I'm not as sick as I think I am. It's okay. I'm going to be okay.* And I was.

Now I keep my emergency pills and my asthma inhaler with me wherever I go. I've attended Mardi Gras parades since I was a child. It's less than optimal to have an anxiety attack while attending a Mardi Gras parade and be trapped by the parade route so you can't get to your meds, and your friends and family are freaking out because they've never seen you like this, and you can't even get the words out to tell them you're having an anxiety attack because you're crying so hard. It was kind of a buzz kill for the atmosphere. Yet the least likely, the least stable person in our group, stepped up and took care of me and knew instinctively what to do to calm me down. So now, even if I'm not carrying a purse, I carry a small pill case, so I have the medication when I need it. I keep some in my car. I keep some in my nightstand. I keep some in my desk, even though I have a home office. Like a Boy Scout, I am prepared.

Onward

My point is that if I can do this, if I can deal with these challenges and still have a good overall quality of life, then it is possible for you to have that, too. Yours won't look like mine, just like mine won't look like yours. Your life will be harder than some, but it will be less hard than others. I have shared my road map to help you navigate living with bipolar disorder. What you do with it is up to you.

I want you to be happy. I want you to be successful, whatever your definition of that is. The illness is only a part of you. It cannot define you *unless you let it*. It is a reason for your thoughts and behaviors; it is not an excuse for them. You are still in the driver's seat. Only you can move your life forward, let it exist as is, or refuse accountability.

It's up to you. If I can do this, then you can do this. The diagnosis is not the end of the world. It is the entrance to a different world that can be better than the one you've lived in until now. Let it be that. Make it that for you. You matter. No illness can ever take that away from you. Never forget that.

Appendix A: Questions from Readers

12 Step Programs and Peer Support Groups

The best resource I've discovered is the Depression and Bipolar Support Alliance, or DBSA. You can find them online at www.DBSAlliance.org. I also recommend the National Alliance on Mental Illness (NAMI) at www.NAMI.org.

Emotions Anonymous (EA) is a 12-Step program for emotions, and there are many peer support programs online.

However, you cannot "twelve step" out of bipolar any more than you can for asthma or diabetes. Bipolar disorder is a medical condition. There are support groups; some people do well with them, and others do not. Before you dive into one, here is my advice:

Find a psychiatrist who is good with meds. This means one who will listen to your symptoms (this includes asking questions about sleep—if they don't ask you about this, find another doctor), make thoughtful recommendations, and have you visit within two to four weeks of starting any new medication. This helps them determine that the dosage is right. With bipolar, anti-depressants are very tricky: not enough and you can be depressed, too much (even by a little) and you can have a manic episode.

Find a therapist that you "mesh" with. This is someone who will be real and objective with you. He/she may be a psychologist, LCSW (licensed clinical social worker), etc. You also have to like and respect them so you feel like you're in a safe environment to spill your guts. They will also give you feedback on any symptoms they observe. For example, mine has told me, "You're talking very fast today." This can be a symptom of mania and hypomania, so she brought that to my attention. Your therapist can evaluate whether or not group therapy is a good fit for you. It's helpful for some yet harmful (depressing) for others.

Group therapy would upset me more than help me, so I do individualized therapy because that's what my therapist recommended. Ask your therapist what they think before you go.

Bipolar Disorder and Menopause

There's a reason you can't find much information on this: "In bipolar disorder, the symptomatology of the illness appears to be altered during the menopause transition; however, data on this subject are lacking..."[17]

Oh, please. There was one survey taken by a total of 22 women with bipolar disorder who were either perimenopausal or postmenopausal.

Here's what I have been able to compile from an article on the subject:

- During the 4 to 5 years of menopausal transition, women have a higher likelihood of depression, anxiety, and bipolar symptoms. Those undergoing hormone therapy have fewer symptoms.

- Rapid cycling may be a new symptom for some women. For those who already experience rapid cycling, there is no significant change.

- There is some extrapolated information related to more general research regarding treatment and medications; I'm not a doctor, so I'm not addressing that.

"More information is needed to assess the best strategy to treat women with bipolar disorder as they get older..."[18] Duh.

Recommended reading: "Girl talk: Bipolar & Menopause" by Elizabeth Forbes, *bp Magazine* editor. http://www.bphope.com/Item.aspx/1099/girl-talk.

Bipolar and Aging

Men and women metabolize medications completely differently with regard to how they absorb the drugs as well as how they are processed in the livers and kidneys.

It seems, according to one study, that *maybe* you need to keep a closer eye on your bone mineral density (BMD) because you *might* be at higher risk for osteoporosis *depending* on what medications you've been on *and* how long you've been on them.

Also, it seems that some of our medications might place us at higher risk for metabolic syndrome as we age. Again, this varies by individual and is dependent on a number of factors. The National Institute of Health (NIH) defines metabolic syndrome as follows:

Metabolic syndrome is a group of conditions that put you at risk for heart disease and diabetes. These conditions are:

- High blood pressure

- High blood glucose, or blood sugar, levels

- High levels of triglycerides, a type of fat, in your blood

- High levels of HDL, the good cholesterol, in your blood

- Too much fat around your waist

Not all doctors agree on the definition or cause of metabolic syndrome. The cause might be insulin resistance. Insulin is a hormone your body produces to help you turn sugar from food into energy for your body. If you are insulin resistant, too much sugar builds up in your blood, setting the stage for disease.[19]

Appendix B: Recommended Reading and Exercises

In alphabetical order by author:

"This Is How" by Augusten Burroughs. There are different editions with two different subtitles. It's the same book. I think I've made enough references in my book that this doesn't require further explanation. It's life changing.

"The Artist's Way' by Julia Cameron. This book is chock full of great exercises for getting out of your head and getting to know yourself. It's also full of great quotes. The Morning Pages are priceless. You need the book to do Morning Pages well. The Morning Pages Workbook is optional.

"Ask and It Is Given" by Esther and Jerry Hicks. The exercises beginning on page 113 and going through page 303 are highly recommended as they correspond to where you are emotionally and are designed to help you gradually improve your attitude and feel better.

"Life Strategies: Doing What Works, Doing What Matters" by Phil McGraw, Ph.D. I started one of my journeys with this book. It's excellent for a crash course in accepting reality. I have found the "Ten Laws of Life" on the back of his book to be true and the strategies effective.

"The Power of Now" by Eckhart Tolle. This is a great book to help you get a handle on thoughts and dealing with the "pain-body." Intrigued? You should be. You can also get his workshops on audio CD. I'm a big fan of "Living the Liberated Life."

Appendix C: Additional Resources

In Case of Emergency

If you are having thoughts of suicide, this is a red flag for an episode You need to 1) get crisis intervention and 2) have your meds adjusted. Take one or more of the following steps immediately:

- Call the National Suicide Prevention Hotline at 988.

- Text the National Suicide Prevention Hotline at 988.

- Visit http://psychcentral.com/helpme.htm for links to chat, phone, and other immediate resources.

- Dial 911 on your phone (in the United States) or go to the hospital or crisis center you've pre-screened for an inpatient psychiatric unit.

- Contact your psychiatrist or therapist. If you cannot reach them **immediately**, then call 911.

Books by Medical Experts

"Bipolar Disorder (A Johns Hopkins Press Health Book)" by Dr. Francis Mark Mondimore. I strongly recommend this book. It's the one my psychiatrist first recommended to me following my diagnosis.

"The Bipolar Survival Guide: What You and Your Family Need to Know" by Dr. David J. Miklowitz. This addresses types of bipolar disorder as well as medications in detail.

"An Unquiet Mind: A Memoir of Moods and Madness" by Dr. Kay Redfield Jamison. This memoir is written by a medical doctor who also suffers from bipolar disorder.

Find a Psychiatric Professional

AMERICAN PSYCHIATRIC ASSOCIATION
https://finder.psychiatry.org/

PSYCHOLOGY TODAY
https://psychiatrists.psychologytoday.com/rms/

Find a Therapist

PSYCHOLOGY TODAY
https://www.psychologytoday.com/

PSYCHCENTRAL
https://psychcentral.com/find-help/

SLIDING SCALE PROVIDERS
https://www.FindTreatment.gov/locator
https://www.needymeds.org/free-clinics

Endnotes

1. Kessler RC, Chiu WT, Demler O, Merikangas KR, Walters EE. Prevalence, severity, and comorbidity of 12-month DSM-IV disorders in the National Comorbidity Survey Replication. Archives of General Psychiatry.2005;62:617–627.

2. Merriam-Webster Dictionary Online, s.v. "recover," http://www.merriam-webster.com/dictionary/recover. (accessed December 1, 2023).

3. Merriam-Webster Dictionary Online, s.v. "recovery," http://www.merriam-webster.com/dictionary/recovery. (accessed December 1, 2023).

4. ChatGPT 3.5, s. v. Define bipolar recovery. https://chat.openai.com/c/0a65cca3-5652-43e1-8f02-4984efa4e216. (accessed March 13, 2023)

5. Gaudiano BA, Weinstock LM, Miller IW. Improving treatment adherence in patients with bipolar disorder and substance abuse: rationale and initial development of a novel psychosocial approach. J Psychiatr Pract. 2011;17(1):5–20.

6. Scott J, Pope M. Nonadherence with mood stabilizers: Prevalence and predictors. J Clin Psychiatry.2002;63:384–90.

7. Gaudiano BA, Weinstock LM, Miller IW. Improving treat-

ment adherence in bipolar disorder: A review of current psychosocial treatment efficacy and recommendations for future treatment development. Behav Modif. 2008;32:267–301.

8. Wood, J. V., Perunovic, W. Q. E., & Lee, J. (2009). Positive thinking: Power for some, peril for others. Psychological Science, 20,860-866.

9. Hicks, Esther and Jerry. Ask and It Is Given: Learning to Manifest Your Desires, 2004 Carlsbad, CA: Hay House, Inc.

10. Hicks, Esther and Jerry. Ask and It Is Given: Learning to Manifest Your Desires, 2004 Carlsbad, CA: Hay House, Inc. Pg. 293-203.

11. U.S. Social Security Administration. Disability Evaluation Under Social Security, 12.00 Mental Disorders – Adult, sec B.3. Depressive, bipolar and related disorders (12.04), sec. E. What are the paragraph B criteria?. https://www.ssa.gov/disability/professionals/bluebook/12.00-MentalDisorders-Adult.htm#12_00E. (accessed December 4, 2024).

12. National Alliance on Mental Illness. Mental Health by the Numbers. https://www.nami.org/mhstats. (accessed March 13, 2024).

13. Dobbs, Bonnie M. Medical Conditions and Driving: A Review of the Scientific Literature (1960-2000). DOT HS 809 690, 2005; Section 12: Psychiatric Diseases. https://one.nhtsa.gov/people/injury/research/medical_condition_driving/pages/Sec12-PsycD.htm. (accessed March 14, 2024)

14. U.S. National Highway Transportation Safety Administration. 2023 ARIDE Participant Guide. 2023:84-85. https://www.nhtsa.gov/sites/nhtsa.gov/files/2023-04/

15941-2023_ARIDE_Participant_Guide-tag.pdf (accessed March 13, 2024).

15. Hill, Napoleon. Think and Grow Rich, 2005 New York: Penguin. Pg. 37.

16. Burroughs, Augusten. This is How: Proven Aid in Overcoming Shyness, Molestation, Fatness, Spinsterhood, Grief, Disease, Lushery, Decrepitude & More. For Young and Old Alike, 2012 New York: St. Martin's Press. Pg. 106.

17. Soares CN, Taylor V. Effects and Management of the Menopausal Transition in Women with Depression and Bipolar Disorder. J Clin Psychiatry 2007;68 (suppl 9):18.

18. Soares CN, Taylor V. Effects and Management of the Menopausal Transition in Women with Depression and Bipolar Disorder. J Clin Psychiatry 2007;68 (suppl 9):20.

19. NIH: National Institute of Diabetes and Digestive and Kidney Disease. http://www.nlm.nih.gov/medlineplus/metabolicsyndrome.html . (accessed March 13, 2024)

Kristi Weldon, CF APMP, is an award-winning author, educator, and marketer dedicated to fostering mental health awareness and empowerment. Unknowingly dealing with bipolar disorder on her own from age 12, she reached out for help only to be punished for doing so. Finally diagnosed at 32, she has been managing her condition successfully for better part of over two decades. With a passion for helping others navigate life's challenges, Kristi brings a unique blend of professional expertise and personal insight to her work. Driven by compassion and a desire to make a difference, Kristi continues to advocate for mental health awareness and accessibility to resources. Through her writing, teaching, and advocacy work, she strives to create a world where individuals feel empowered to live their best lives. As an author, Kristi has leveraged her experiences and expertise to empower others on their journey toward mental wellness. Her book, "Help! I'm Bipolar: Life Hacks for Us," is a testament to her commitment to providing practical guidance and support to those living with bipolar disorder. Kristi was also a dedicated educator, sharing her English language knowledge and expertise with students. She received a special award for starting a Choose Your Attitude Committee for faculty and staff at one of the toughest schools in the nation. Kristi's innovative strategies and creative approach have earned her recognition and accolades within corporate America. As a Foundations Certified Member of the Association of Proposal Management Professionals (CF APMP), Kristi has demonstrated her commitment to excellence in marketing and communication. She also has served as chair for APMP's Mental Health Affinity Group. She has presented to the APMP, Romance Writers of America (RWA), Atlanta Writers Club, and loves to volunteer in her spare time. Outside of her non-fiction work, Kristi writes small-town contemporary romance under the pen name Kristine Bria and explores erotica under the pseudonym Kristi Hancock.

Connect with Kristi Weldon:
www.RealPositiveAttitude.com
https://www.facebook.com/HelpImBipolar.book

For inquiries, speaking engagements, or collaborations, please contact:
Kristi@RealPositiveAttitude.com

www.ingramcontent.com/pod-product-compliance
Lightning Source LLC
Chambersburg PA
CBHW071712020426
42333CB00017B/2241